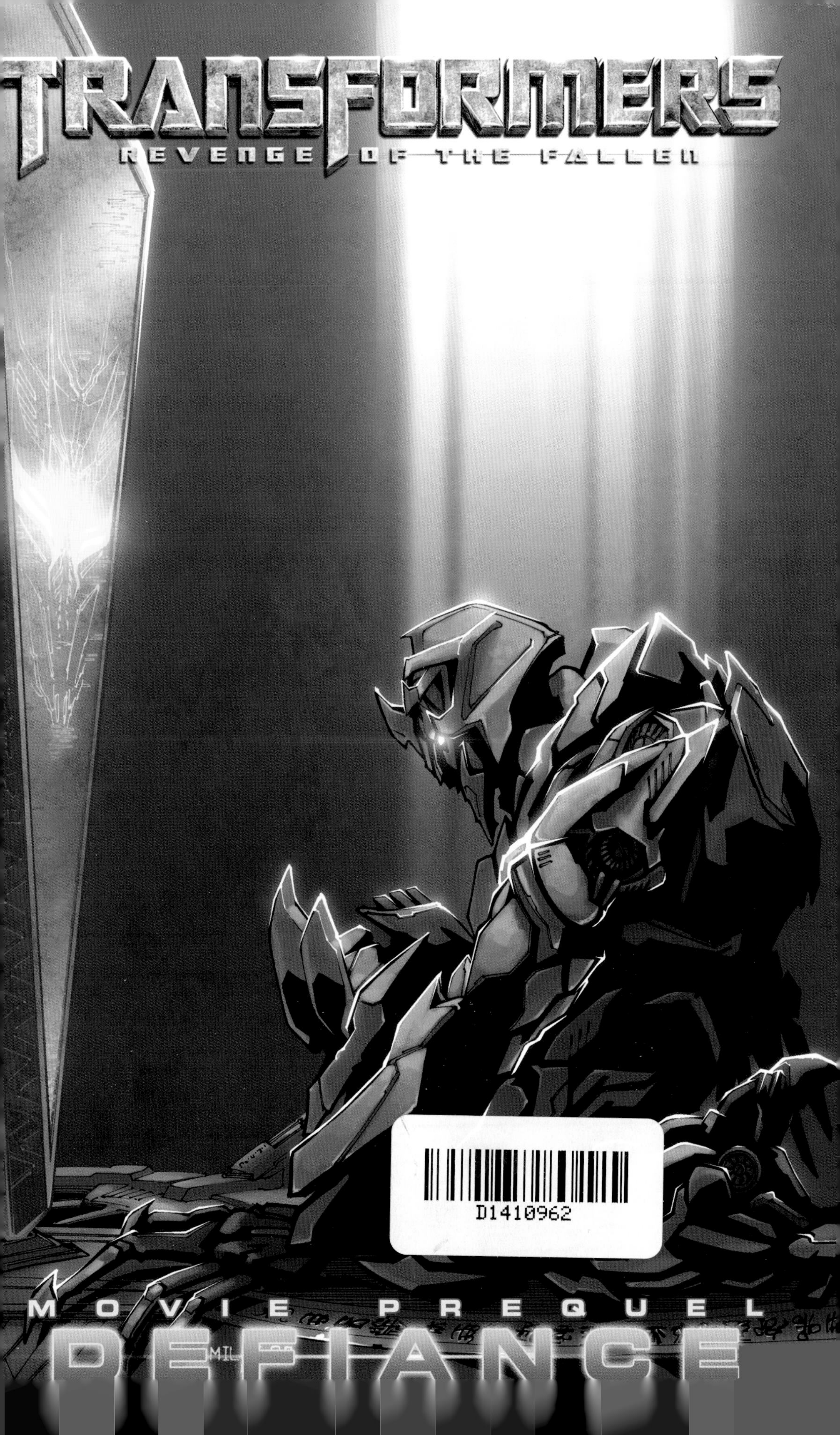
TRANSFORMERS
REVENGE OF THE FALLEN
MOVIE PREQUEL
DEFIANCE

TRANSFORMERS: REVENGE OF THE FALLEN:
DEFIANCE

WRITTEN BY: **CHRIS MOWRY**

PENCILS BY: **DAN KHANNA, ANDREW GRIFFITH, & DON FIGUEROA**

INKS BY: **ANDREW GRIFFITH & JOHN WYCOUGH**

COLORS BY: **JOSH PEREZ**

LETTERS BY: **CHRIS MOWRY**

EDITS BY: **ANDY SCHMIDT & DENTON J. TIPTON**

COLLECTION EDITS BY: **JUSTIN EISINGER & MARIAH HUEHNER**

COLLECTION DESIGN BY: **CHRIS MOWRY & ROBBIE ROBBINS**

Special thanks to Hasbro's Aaron Archer, Michael Kelly, Amie Lozanzki, Val Roca, Ed Lane, Michael Provost,
Erin Hillman, Samantha Lomow, and Michael Verecchia for their invaluable assistance.

IDW Pu
Ope
Ted Adams, Chief Executive
Greg Goldstein, Chief Operating
Matthew Ruzicka, CPA, Chief Financia
Alan Payne, VP o
AnnaMaria White, Marketing & PR M
Lorelei Bunjes, Dir. of Digital S
Marci Hubbard, Executive A
Alonzo Simon, Shipping M

E
Chris Ryall, Publisher/Editor-i
Scott Dunbier, Editor, Special P
Andy Schmidt, Senio
Justin Eisinge
Kris Oprisko, Editor/Fore
Denton J. Tipton
Tom Waltz
Mariah Huehner, Associate

Robbie Robbins, EVP/Sr. Graph
Ben Templesmith, Artist/D
Neil Uyetake, Art D
Chris Mowry, Graphi

 Licensed by:

ISBN: 978-1-60010-457-2
12 11 10 09   1 2 3 4

To discuss this issue of *Transformers*, join the IDW Insiders, or
to check out exclusive Web offers, check out our site:

WWW.IDWPUBLISHING.COM

CHAPTER ONE

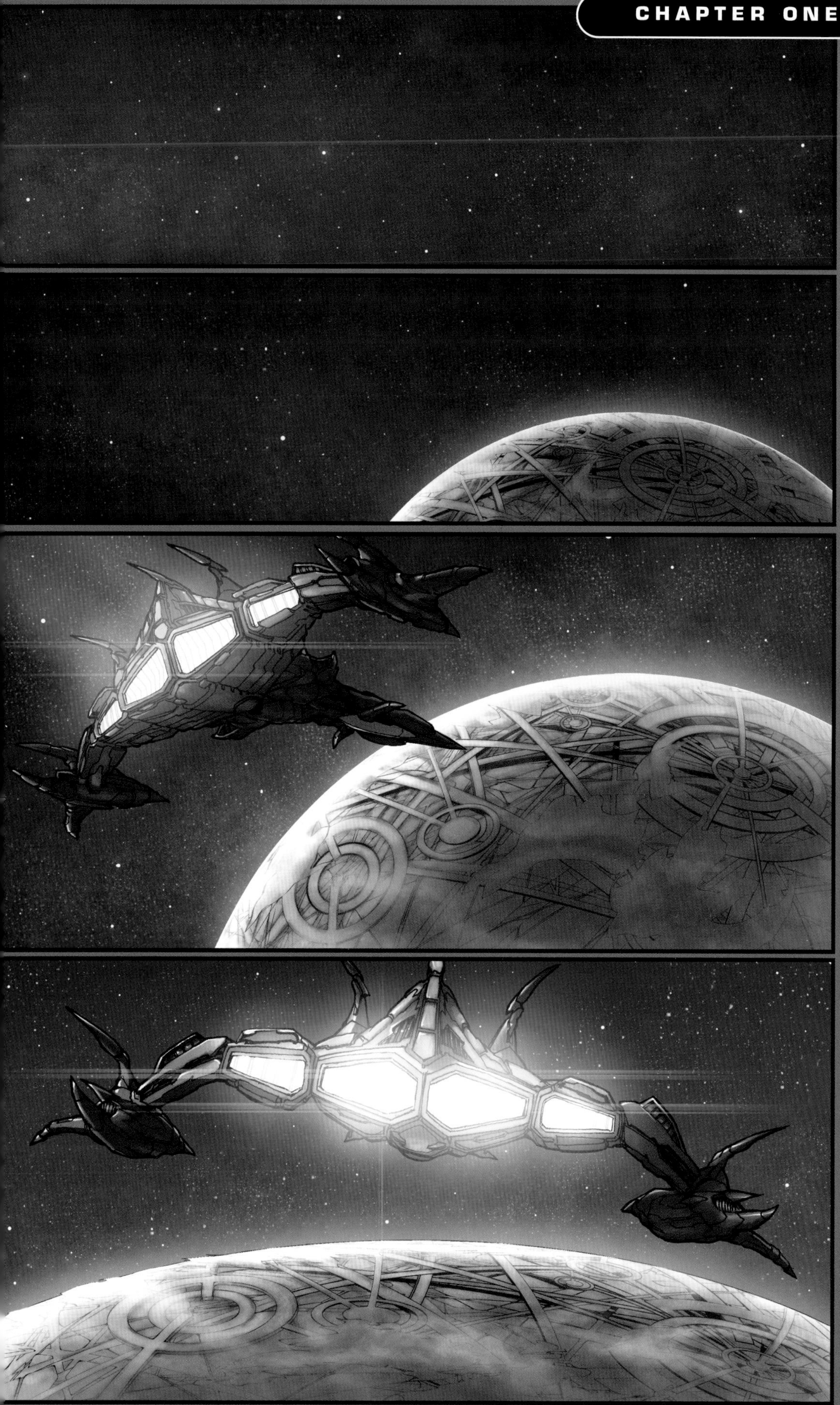

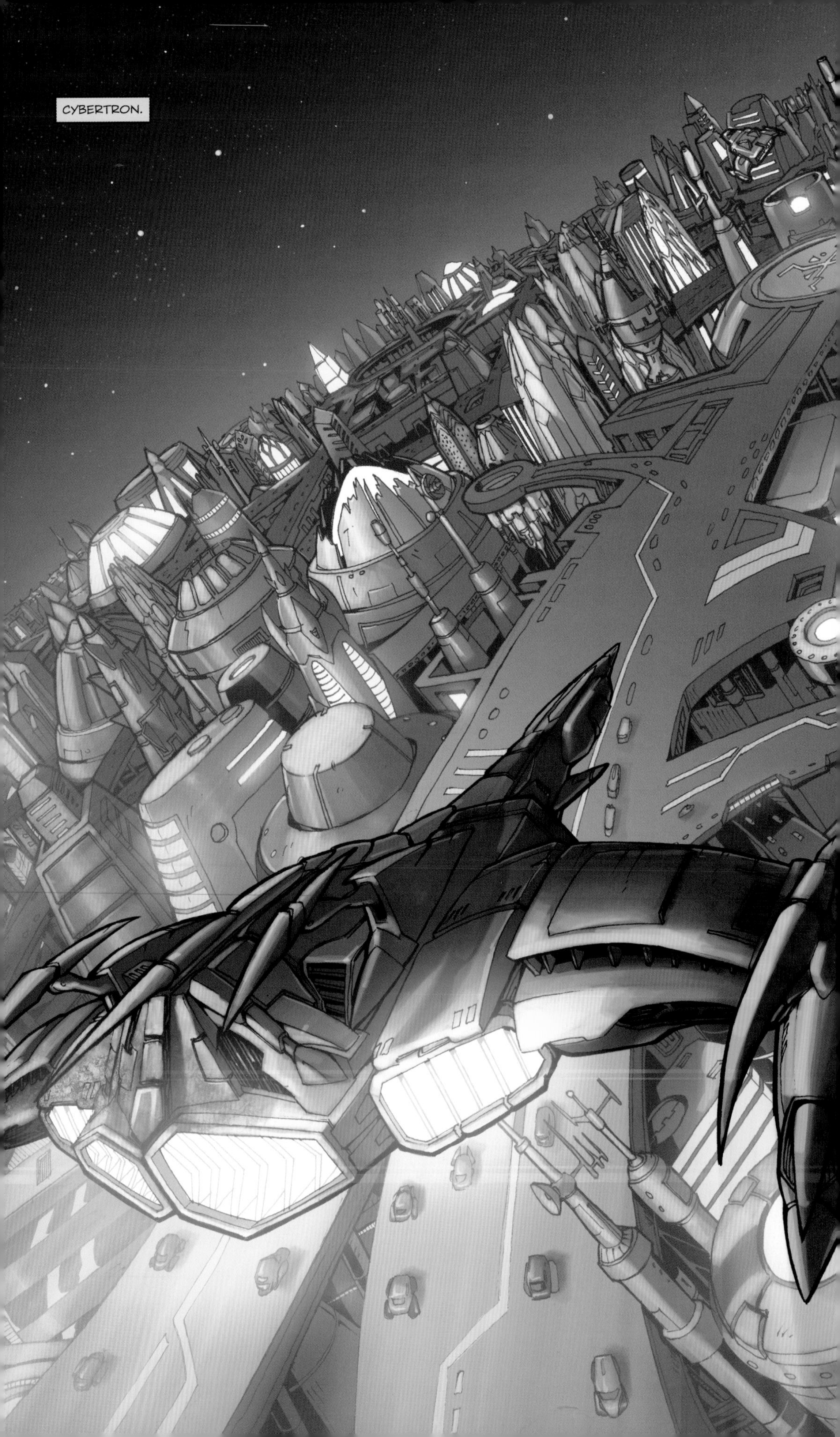
CYBERTRON.

MANY, MANY YEARS AGO.

COMMANDER STARSCREAM, HOW MAY I BE OF SERVICE?

AH, FIRST OFFICER RATCHET.

TROUBLE AT THE ESHEMS NEBULA AGAIN, COMMANDER?

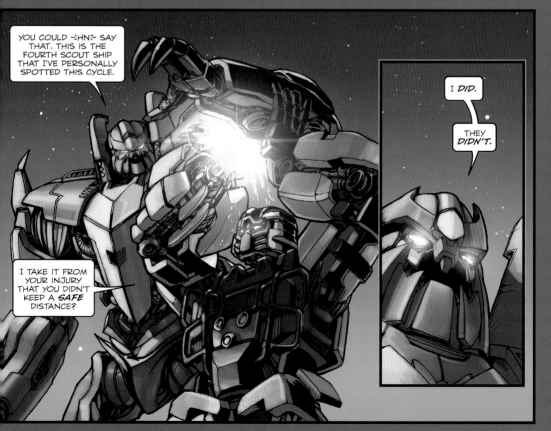

YOU COULD -∺HN∺- SAY THAT. THIS IS THE FOURTH SCOUT SHIP THAT I'VE PERSONALLY SPOTTED THIS CYCLE.

I TAKE IT FROM YOUR INJURY THAT YOU DIDN'T KEEP A *SAFE* DISTANCE?

I *DID.*

THEY *DIDN'T.*

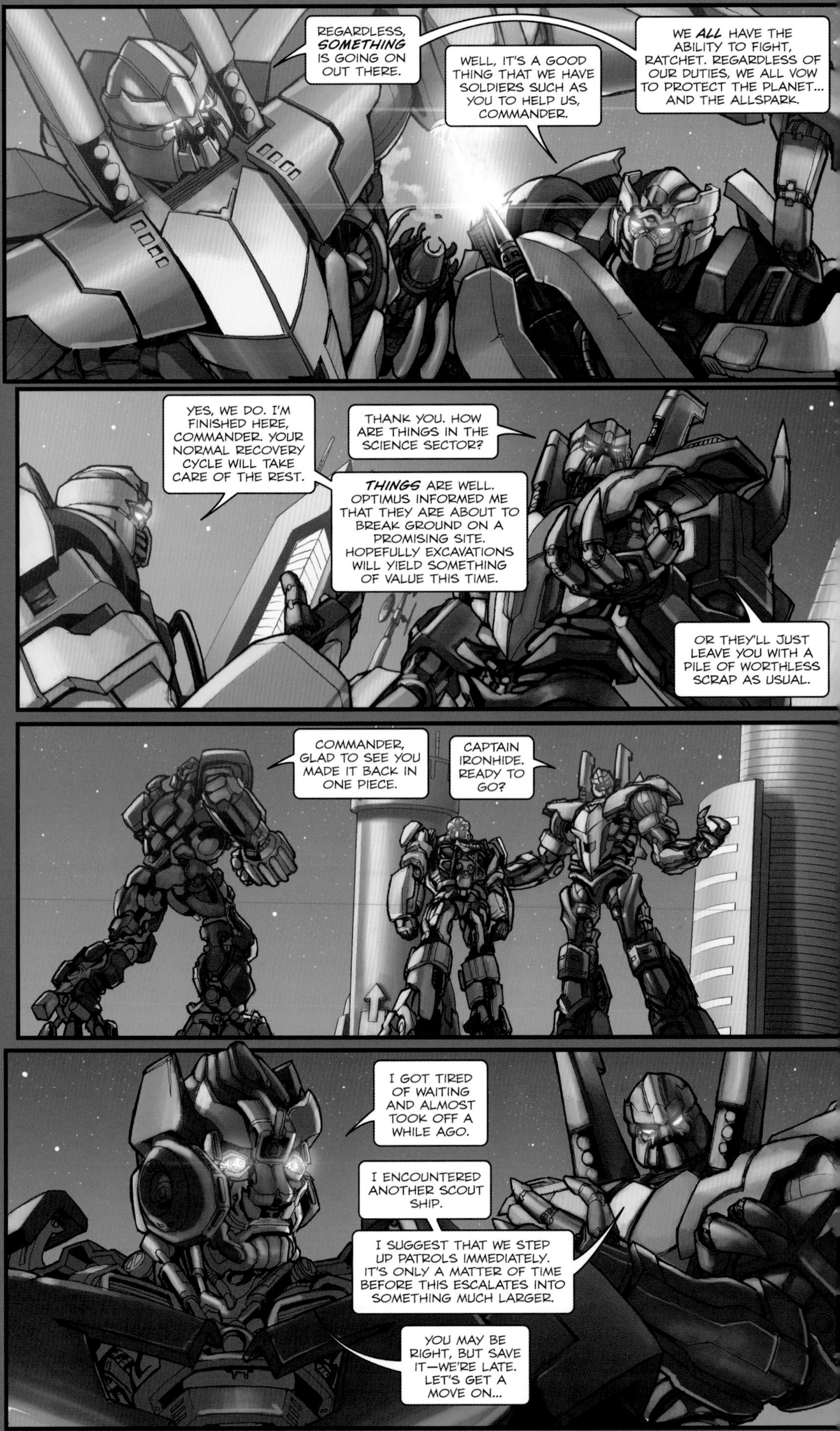
REGARDLESS, SOMETHING IS GOING ON OUT THERE.
WELL, IT'S A GOOD THING THAT WE HAVE SOLDIERS SUCH AS YOU TO HELP US, COMMANDER.
WE ALL HAVE THE ABILITY TO FIGHT, RATCHET. REGARDLESS OF OUR DUTIES, WE ALL VOW TO PROTECT THE PLANET... AND THE ALLSPARK.
YES, WE DO. I'M FINISHED HERE, COMMANDER. YOUR NORMAL RECOVERY CYCLE WILL TAKE CARE OF THE REST.
THANK YOU. HOW ARE THINGS IN THE SCIENCE SECTOR?
THINGS ARE WELL. OPTIMUS INFORMED ME THAT THEY ARE ABOUT TO BREAK GROUND ON A PROMISING SITE. HOPEFULLY EXCAVATIONS WILL YIELD SOMETHING OF VALUE THIS TIME.
OR THEY'LL JUST LEAVE YOU WITH A PILE OF WORTHLESS SCRAP AS USUAL.
COMMANDER, GLAD TO SEE YOU MADE IT BACK IN ONE PIECE.
CAPTAIN IRONHIDE. READY TO GO?
I GOT TIRED OF WAITING AND ALMOST TOOK OFF A WHILE AGO.
I ENCOUNTERED ANOTHER SCOUT SHIP.
I SUGGEST THAT WE STEP UP PATROLS IMMEDIATELY. IT'S ONLY A MATTER OF TIME BEFORE THIS ESCALATES INTO SOMETHING MUCH LARGER.
YOU MAY BE RIGHT, BUT SAVE IT—WE'RE LATE. LET'S GET A MOVE ON...

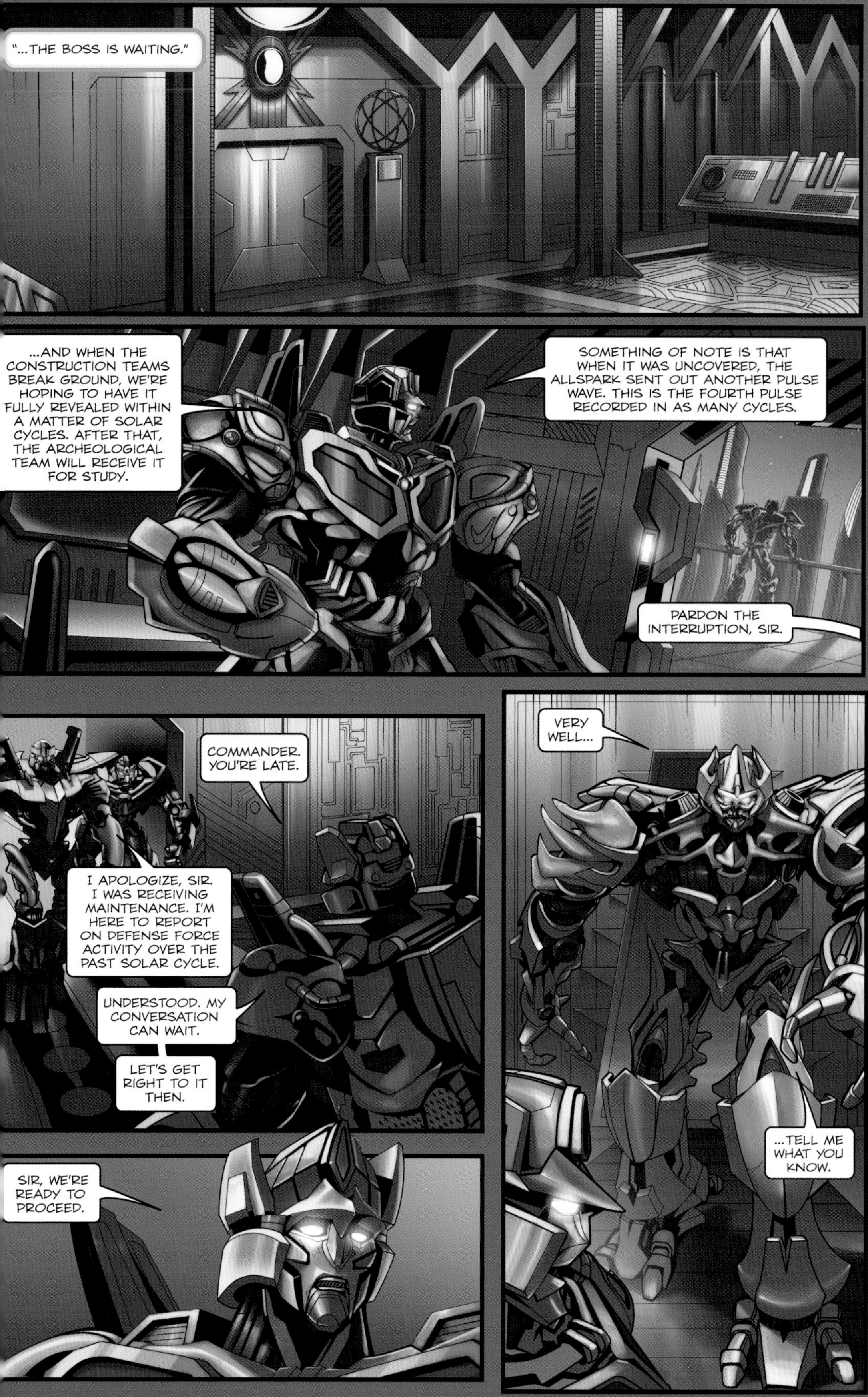
"...THE BOSS IS WAITING."
...AND WHEN THE CONSTRUCTION TEAMS BREAK GROUND, WE'RE HOPING TO HAVE IT FULLY REVEALED WITHIN A MATTER OF SOLAR CYCLES. AFTER THAT, THE ARCHEOLOGICAL TEAM WILL RECEIVE IT FOR STUDY.
SOMETHING OF NOTE IS THAT WHEN IT WAS UNCOVERED, THE ALLSPARK SENT OUT ANOTHER PULSE WAVE. THIS IS THE FOURTH PULSE RECORDED IN AS MANY CYCLES.
PARDON THE INTERRUPTION, SIR.
COMMANDER. YOU'RE LATE.
I APOLOGIZE, SIR. I WAS RECEIVING MAINTENANCE. I'M HERE TO REPORT ON DEFENSE FORCE ACTIVITY OVER THE PAST SOLAR CYCLE.
UNDERSTOOD. MY CONVERSATION CAN WAIT.
LET'S GET RIGHT TO IT THEN.
SIR, WE'RE READY TO PROCEED.
VERY WELL...
...TELL ME WHAT YOU KNOW.

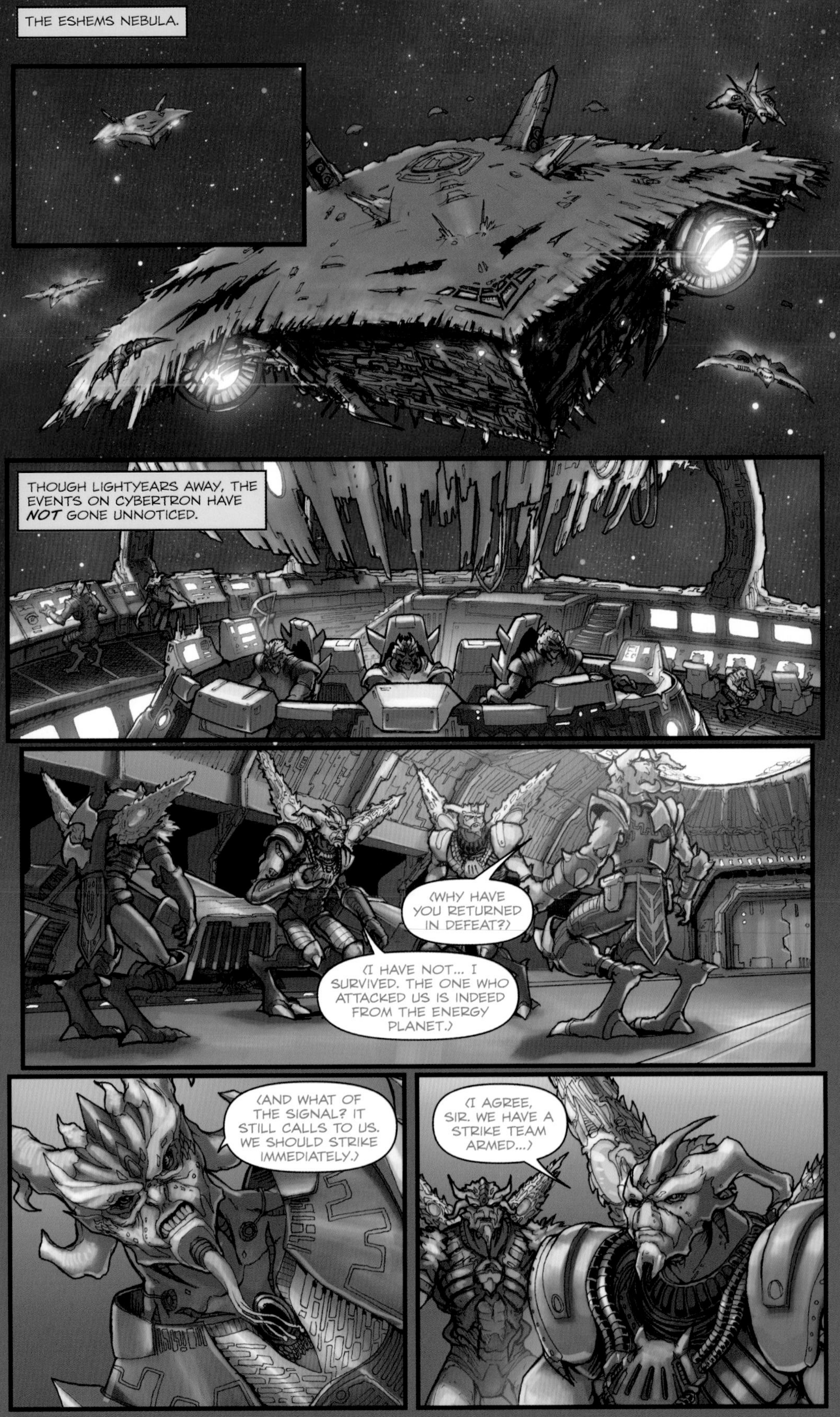
THE ESHEMS NEBULA.
THOUGH LIGHTYEARS AWAY, THE EVENTS ON CYBERTRON HAVE *NOT* GONE UNNOTICED.
(WHY HAVE YOU RETURNED IN DEFEAT?)
(I HAVE NOT... I SURVIVED. THE ONE WHO ATTACKED US IS INDEED FROM THE ENERGY PLANET.)
(AND WHAT OF THE SIGNAL? IT STILL CALLS TO US. WE SHOULD STRIKE IMMEDIATELY.)
(I AGREE, SIR. WE HAVE A STRIKE TEAM ARMED...)

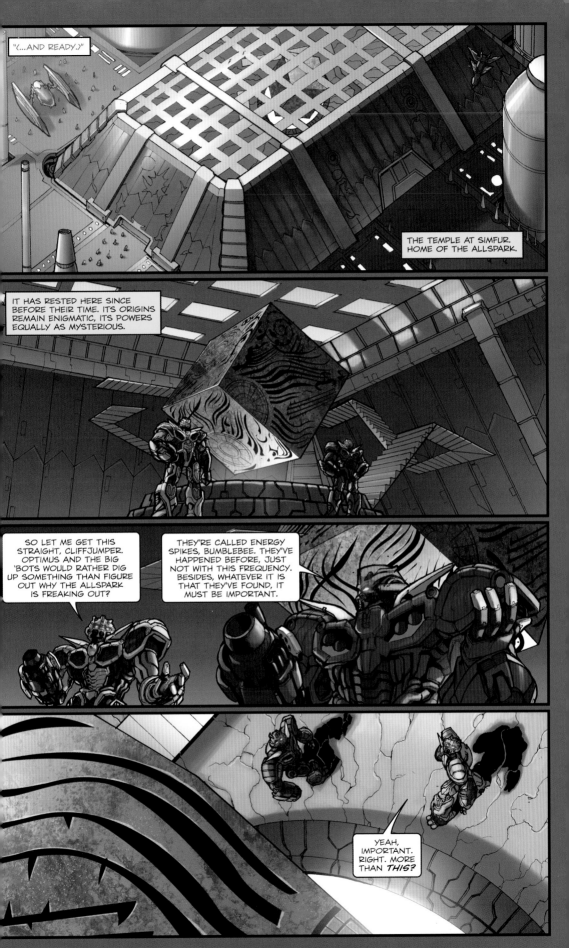

"(...AND READY.)"

THE TEMPLE AT SIMFUR. HOME OF THE ALLSPARK.

IT HAS RESTED HERE SINCE BEFORE THEIR TIME. ITS ORIGINS REMAIN ENIGMATIC, ITS POWERS EQUALLY AS MYSTERIOUS.

SO LET ME GET THIS STRAIGHT, CLIFFJUMPER. OPTIMUS AND THE BIG 'BOTS WOULD RATHER DIG UP SOMETHING THAN FIGURE OUT WHY THE ALLSPARK IS FREAKING OUT?

THEY'RE CALLED ENERGY SPIKES, BUMBLEBEE. THEY'VE HAPPENED BEFORE, JUST NOT WITH THIS FREQUENCY. BESIDES, WHATEVER IT IS THAT THEY'VE FOUND, IT MUST BE IMPORTANT.

YEAH, IMPORTANT. RIGHT. MORE THAN *THIS*?

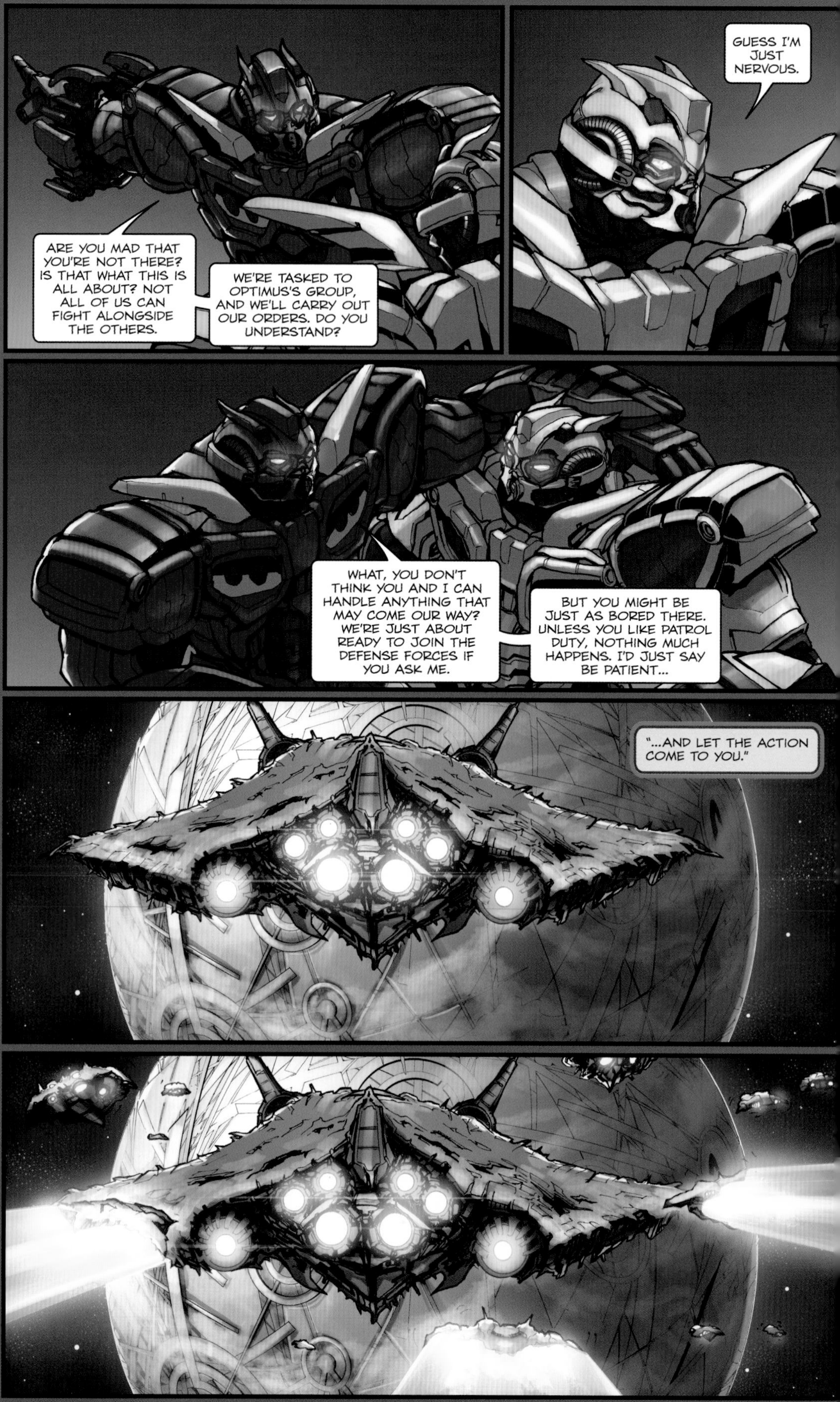
GUESS I'M JUST NERVOUS.
ARE YOU MAD THAT YOU'RE NOT THERE? IS THAT WHAT THIS IS ALL ABOUT? NOT ALL OF US CAN FIGHT ALONGSIDE THE OTHERS.
WE'RE TASKED TO OPTIMUS'S GROUP, AND WE'LL CARRY OUT OUR ORDERS. DO YOU UNDERSTAND?
WHAT, YOU DON'T THINK YOU AND I CAN HANDLE ANYTHING THAT MAY COME OUR WAY? WE'RE JUST ABOUT READY TO JOIN THE DEFENSE FORCES IF YOU ASK ME.
BUT YOU MIGHT BE JUST AS BORED THERE. UNLESS YOU LIKE PATROL DUTY, NOTHING MUCH HAPPENS. I'D JUST SAY BE PATIENT...
"...AND LET THE ACTION COME TO YOU."

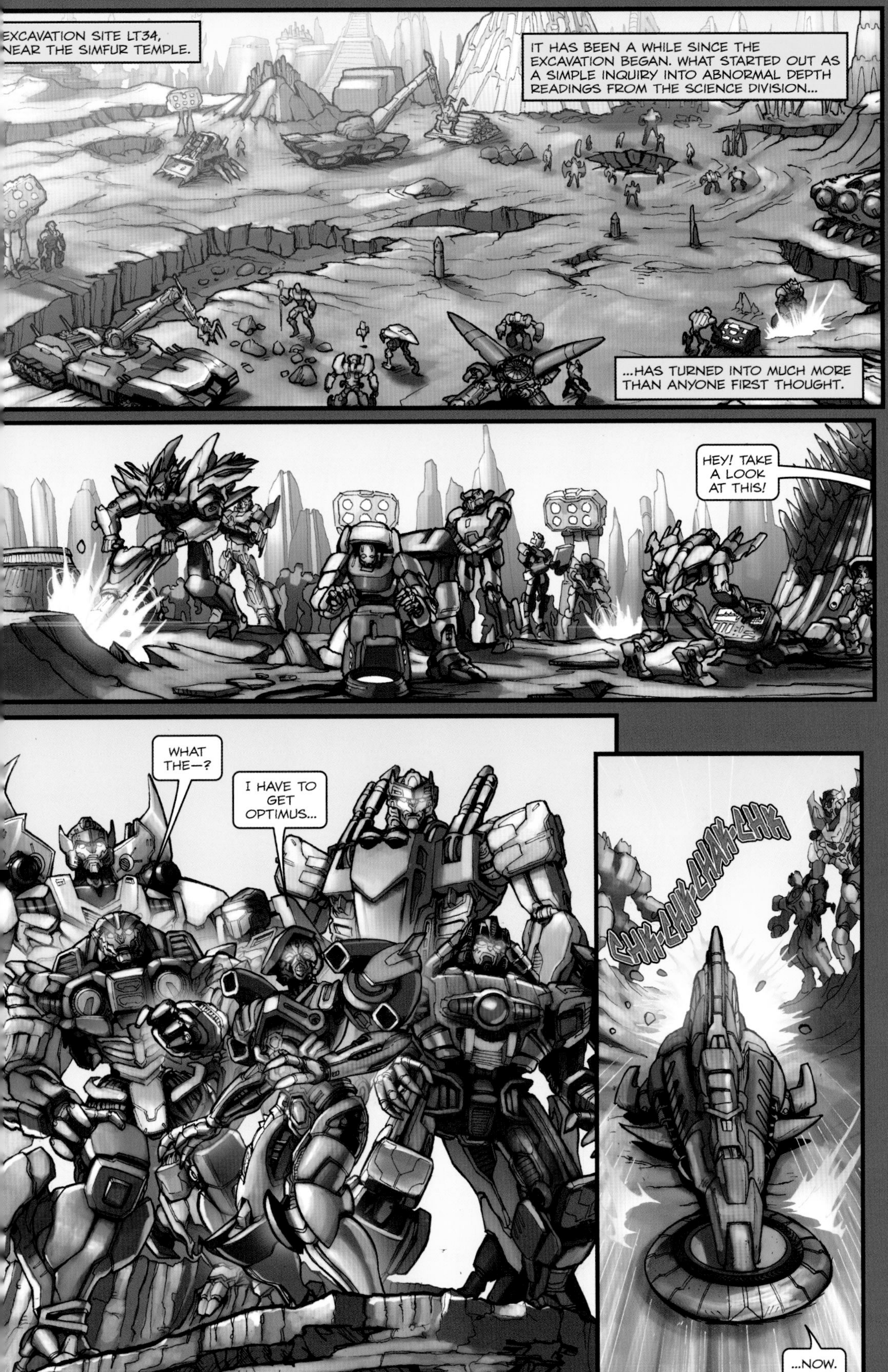
EXCAVATION SITE LT34, NEAR THE SIMFUR TEMPLE.
IT HAS BEEN A WHILE SINCE THE EXCAVATION BEGAN. WHAT STARTED OUT AS A SIMPLE INQUIRY INTO ABNORMAL DEPTH READINGS FROM THE SCIENCE DIVISION...
...HAS TURNED INTO MUCH MORE THAN ANYONE FIRST THOUGHT.
HEY! TAKE A LOOK AT THIS!
WHAT THE--?
I HAVE TO GET OPTIMUS...
CHK-CHK-CHAK-CHK
...NOW.

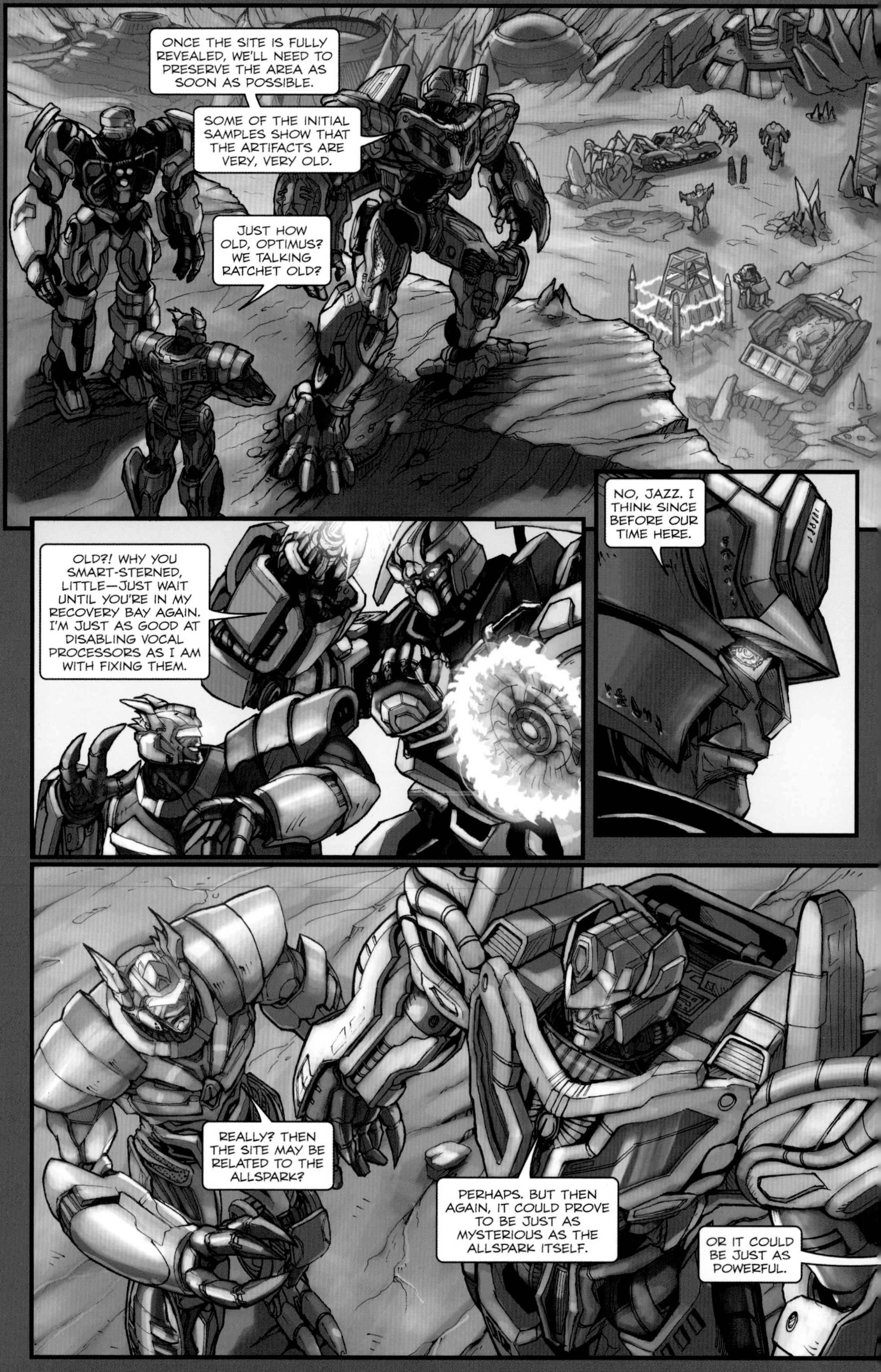
ONCE THE SITE IS FULLY REVEALED, WE'LL NEED TO PRESERVE THE AREA AS SOON AS POSSIBLE.
SOME OF THE INITIAL SAMPLES SHOW THAT THE ARTIFACTS ARE VERY, VERY OLD.
JUST HOW OLD, OPTIMUS? WE TALKING RATCHET OLD?
OLD?! WHY YOU SMART-STERNED, LITTLE—JUST WAIT UNTIL YOU'RE IN MY RECOVERY BAY AGAIN. I'M JUST AS GOOD AT DISABLING VOCAL PROCESSORS AS I AM WITH FIXING THEM.
NO, JAZZ. I THINK SINCE BEFORE OUR TIME HERE.
REALLY? THEN THE SITE MAY BE RELATED TO THE ALLSPARK?
PERHAPS. BUT THEN AGAIN, IT COULD PROVE TO BE JUST AS MYSTERIOUS AS THE ALLSPARK ITSELF.
OR IT COULD BE JUST AS POWERFUL.

TELL ME, OPTIMUS. WHAT DO YOU THINK IT IS?

I CAN'T TELL, SIR. BUT IF I HAD TO GUESS, I'D SAY THAT IT'S POSSIBLY A LINK TO OUR PAST.

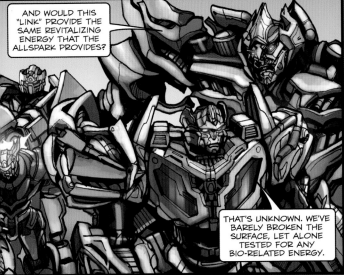

AND WOULD THIS "LINK" PROVIDE THE SAME REVITALIZING ENERGY THAT THE ALLSPARK PROVIDES?

THAT'S UNKNOWN. WE'VE BARELY BROKEN THE SURFACE, LET ALONE TESTED FOR ANY BIO-RELATED ENERGY.

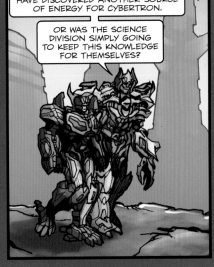

AND WHY IS THAT? THE ALLSPARK HAS BEEN EMITTING ENERGY AT A HIGHER RATE LATELY, AND YOU HAVE YET TO TEST THIS NEW SITE FOR THE SAME ENERGY READINGS? WE COULD HAVE DISCOVERED ANOTHER SOURCE OF ENERGY FOR CYBERTRON.

OR WAS THE SCIENCE DIVISION SIMPLY GOING TO KEEP THIS KNOWLEDGE FOR THEMSELVES?

PARDON ME, SIR, BUT THE SCIENCE DIVISION HAS RIGHTS OVER ALL DISCOVERIES BOTH BIOLOGICAL AND ARCHEOLOGICAL. NOT ONLY COULD THE SUBJECT MATTER BE DELICATE AND FRAGILE, IT COULD BE DANGEROUS AS WELL.

REMEMBER THAT IT IS MY ARMY AND I THAT KEEP US PROTECTED HERE, OPTIMUS. YOU ARE TO REPORT ANY HAZARDOUS FINDINGS TO ME IMMEDIATELY SO THAT THE DEFENSE FORCES CAN DEAL WITH IT APPROPRIATELY.

I UNDERSTAND, SIR. HOWEVER, I RESPECTIVELY DISAGREE WITH YOUR DECISIONS. THERE HAVE BEEN NUMEROUS INCIDENTS IN WHICH FINDINGS HAVE BEEN REPORTED ONLY TO BE TREATED AS HOSTILE ACTIONS BY YOUR DEFENSE FORCES.

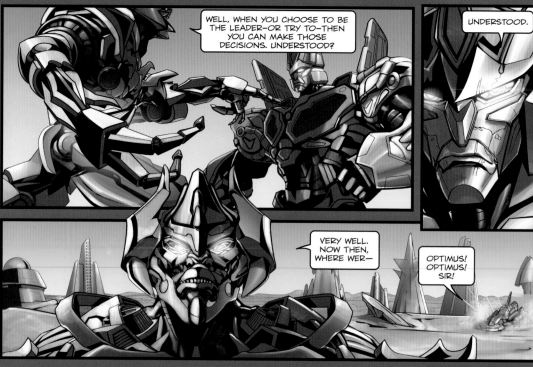

WELL, WHEN YOU CHOOSE TO BE THE LEADER—OR TRY TO—THEN YOU CAN MAKE THOSE DECISIONS. UNDERSTOOD?

UNDERSTOOD.

VERY WELL. NOW THEN, WHERE WER—

OPTIMUS! OPTIMUS! SIR!

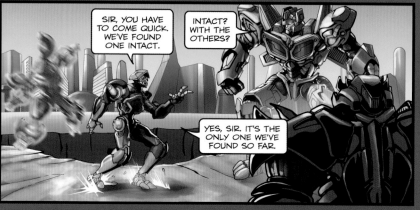

SIR, YOU HAVE TO COME QUICK. WE'VE FOUND ONE INTACT.

INTACT? WITH THE OTHERS?

YES, SIR. IT'S THE ONLY ONE WE'VE FOUND SO FAR.

ONLY ONE, *WHAT?*

WELL, SIR, WE DON'T KNOW WHAT THEY ARE. THE SITE IS STILL FAR FROM BEING FULLY REVEALED, BUT SO FAR THE OBJECTS ALL SHOW A PATTERN.

OBJECTS? JUST WHAT KIND OF OBJECTS?

WELL, THEY'RE BROKEN, EXCEPT THE ONE. WHY DON'T YOU COME SEE FOR YOURSELF?

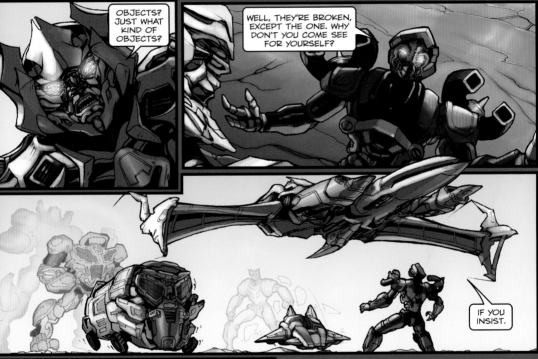

IF YOU INSIST.

MEGATRON, DO NOT TOUCH ANYTHING.

REMARKABLE.

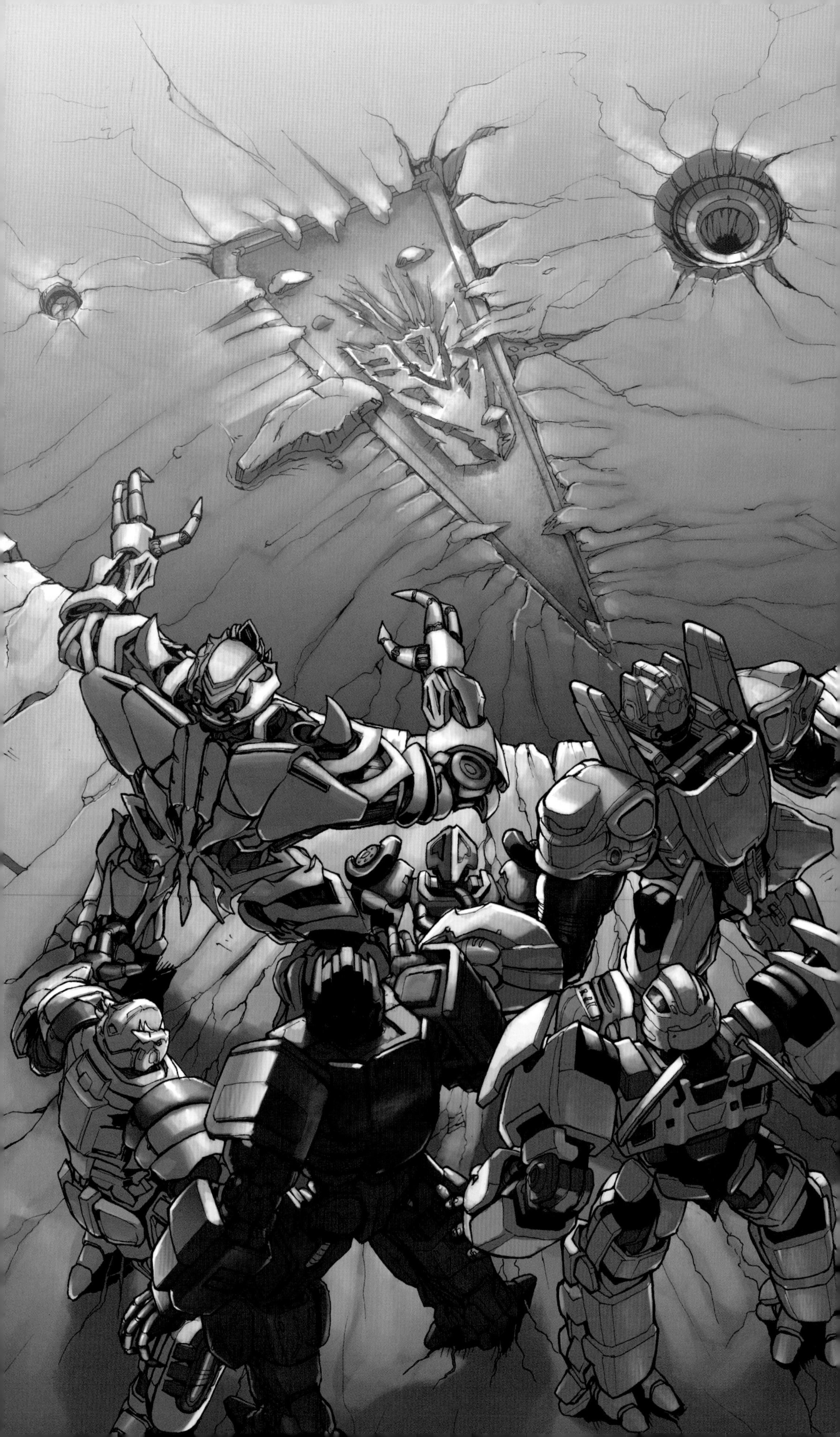

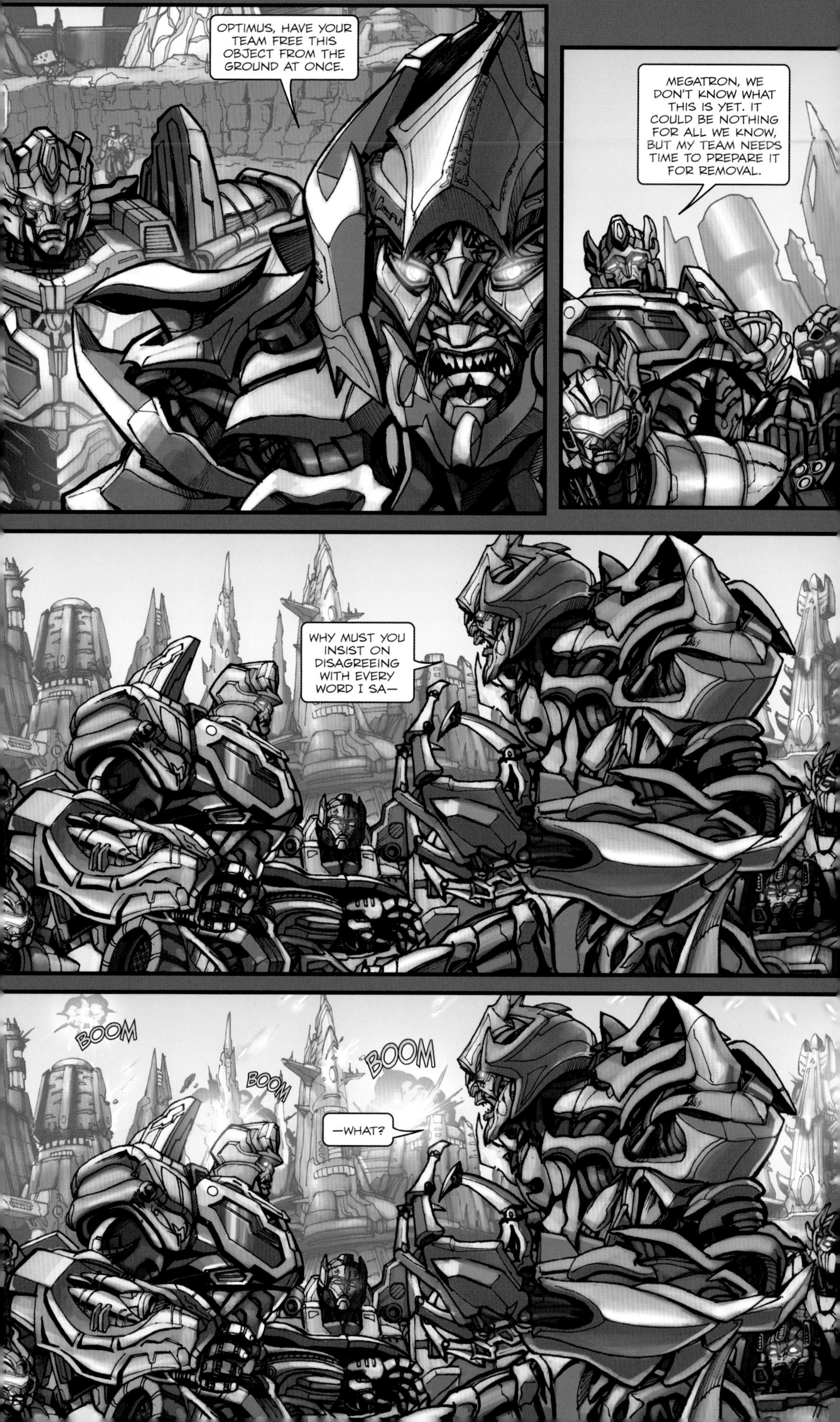
OPTIMUS, HAVE YOUR TEAM FREE THIS OBJECT FROM THE GROUND AT ONCE.
MEGATRON, WE DON'T KNOW WHAT THIS IS YET. IT COULD BE NOTHING FOR ALL WE KNOW, BUT MY TEAM NEEDS TIME TO PREPARE IT FOR REMOVAL.
WHY MUST YOU INSIST ON DISAGREEING WITH EVERY WORD I SA—
BOOM
BOOM
BOOM
—WHAT?

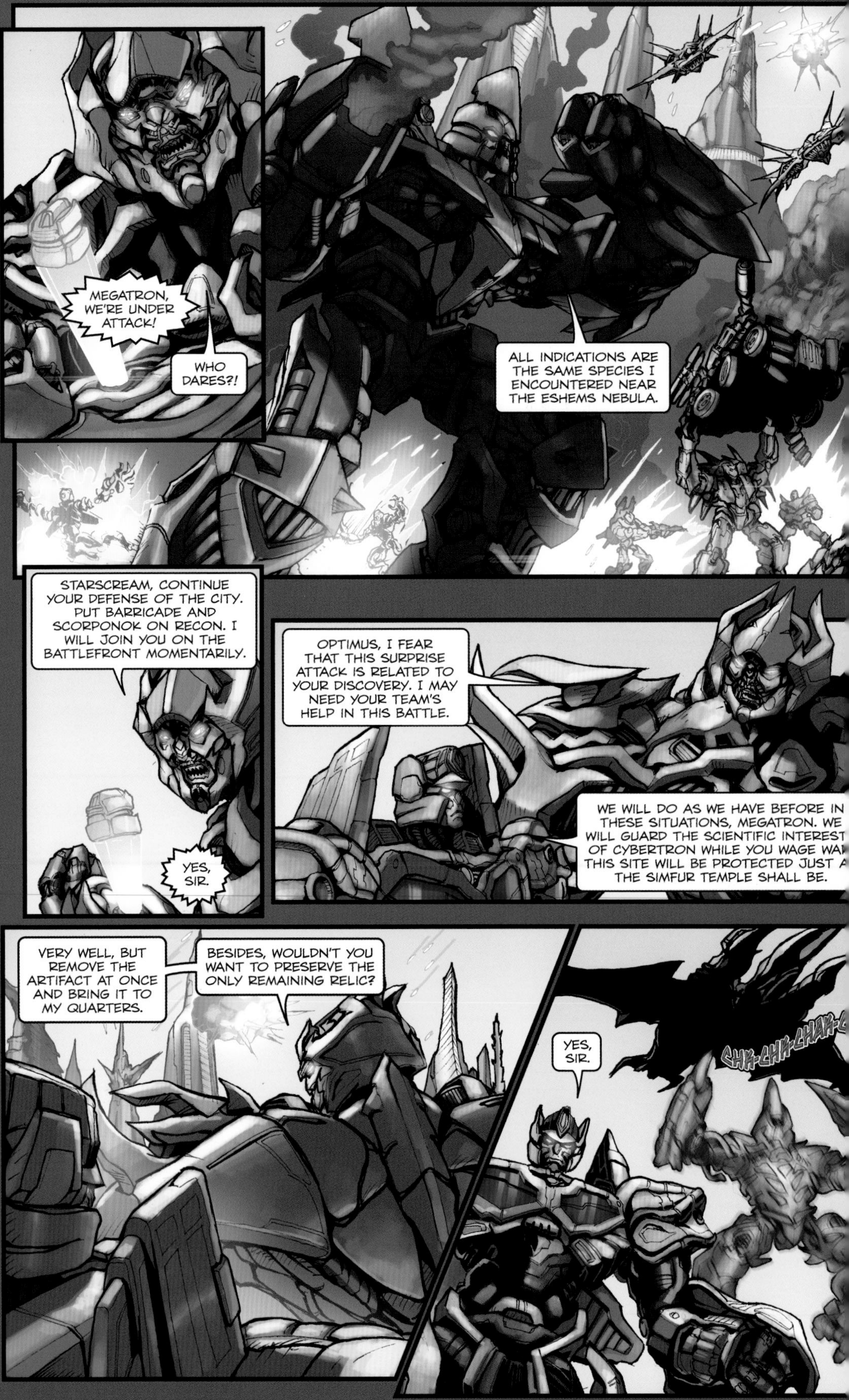
MEGATRON, WE'RE UNDER ATTACK!
WHO DARES?!
ALL INDICATIONS ARE THE SAME SPECIES I ENCOUNTERED NEAR THE ESHEMS NEBULA.
STARSCREAM, CONTINUE YOUR DEFENSE OF THE CITY. PUT BARRICADE AND SCORPONOK ON RECON. I WILL JOIN YOU ON THE BATTLEFRONT MOMENTARILY.
YES, SIR.
OPTIMUS, I FEAR THAT THIS SURPRISE ATTACK IS RELATED TO YOUR DISCOVERY. I MAY NEED YOUR TEAM'S HELP IN THIS BATTLE.
WE WILL DO AS WE HAVE BEFORE IN THESE SITUATIONS, MEGATRON. WE WILL GUARD THE SCIENTIFIC INTEREST OF CYBERTRON WHILE YOU WAGE WA THIS SITE WILL BE PROTECTED JUST A THE SIMFUR TEMPLE SHALL BE.
VERY WELL, BUT REMOVE THE ARTIFACT AT ONCE AND BRING IT TO MY QUARTERS.
BESIDES, WOULDN'T YOU WANT TO PRESERVE THE ONLY REMAINING RELIC?
YES, SIR.
CHK-CHK-CHAK-

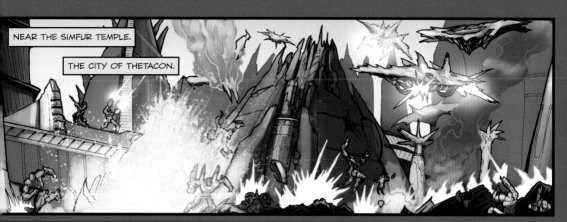

NEAR THE SIMFUR TEMPLE.

THE CITY OF THETACON.

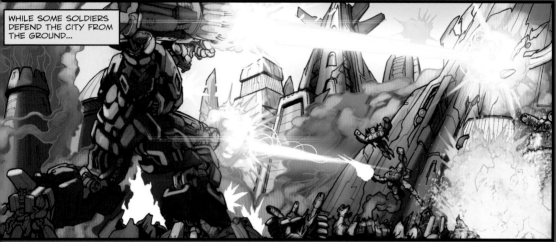

WHILE SOME SOLDIERS DEFEND THE CITY FROM THE GROUND...

...OTHERS LASH OUT IN THE SKY ABOVE.

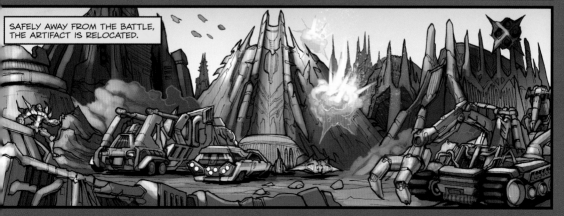

SAFELY AWAY FROM THE BATTLE, THE ARTIFACT IS RELOCATED.

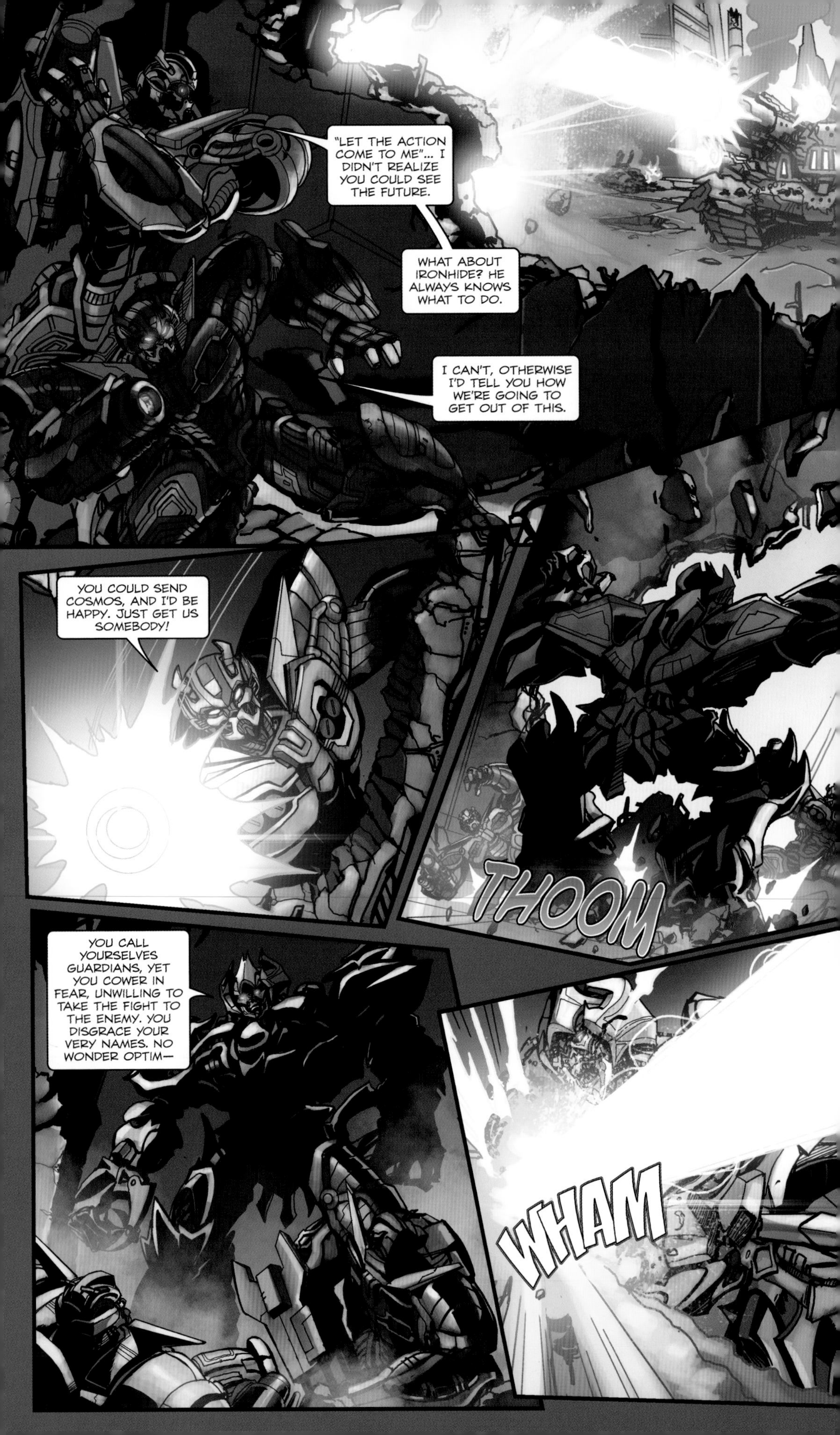
"LET THE ACTION COME TO ME"... I DIDN'T REALIZE YOU COULD SEE THE FUTURE.
WHAT ABOUT IRONHIDE? HE ALWAYS KNOWS WHAT TO DO.
I CAN'T, OTHERWISE I'D TELL YOU HOW WE'RE GOING TO GET OUT OF THIS.
YOU COULD SEND COSMOS, AND I'D BE HAPPY. JUST GET US SOMEBODY!
THOOM
YOU CALL YOURSELVES GUARDIANS, YET YOU COWER IN FEAR, UNWILLING TO TAKE THE FIGHT TO THE ENEMY. YOU DISGRACE YOUR VERY NAMES. NO WONDER OPTIM—
WHAM

THUD
SHNNG

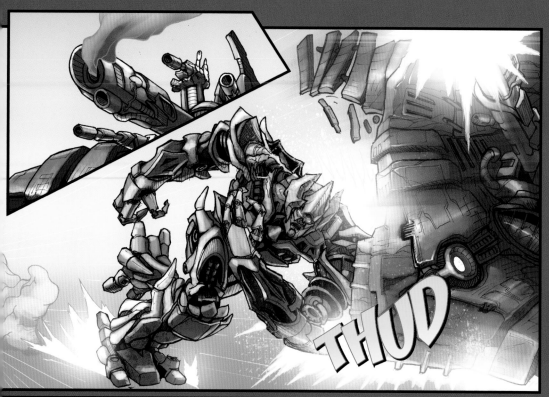

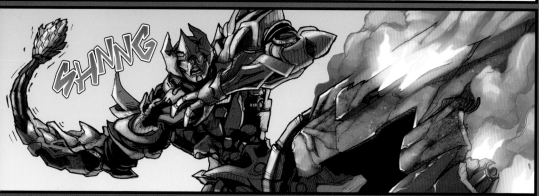

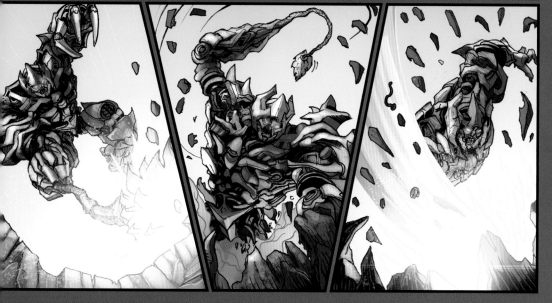

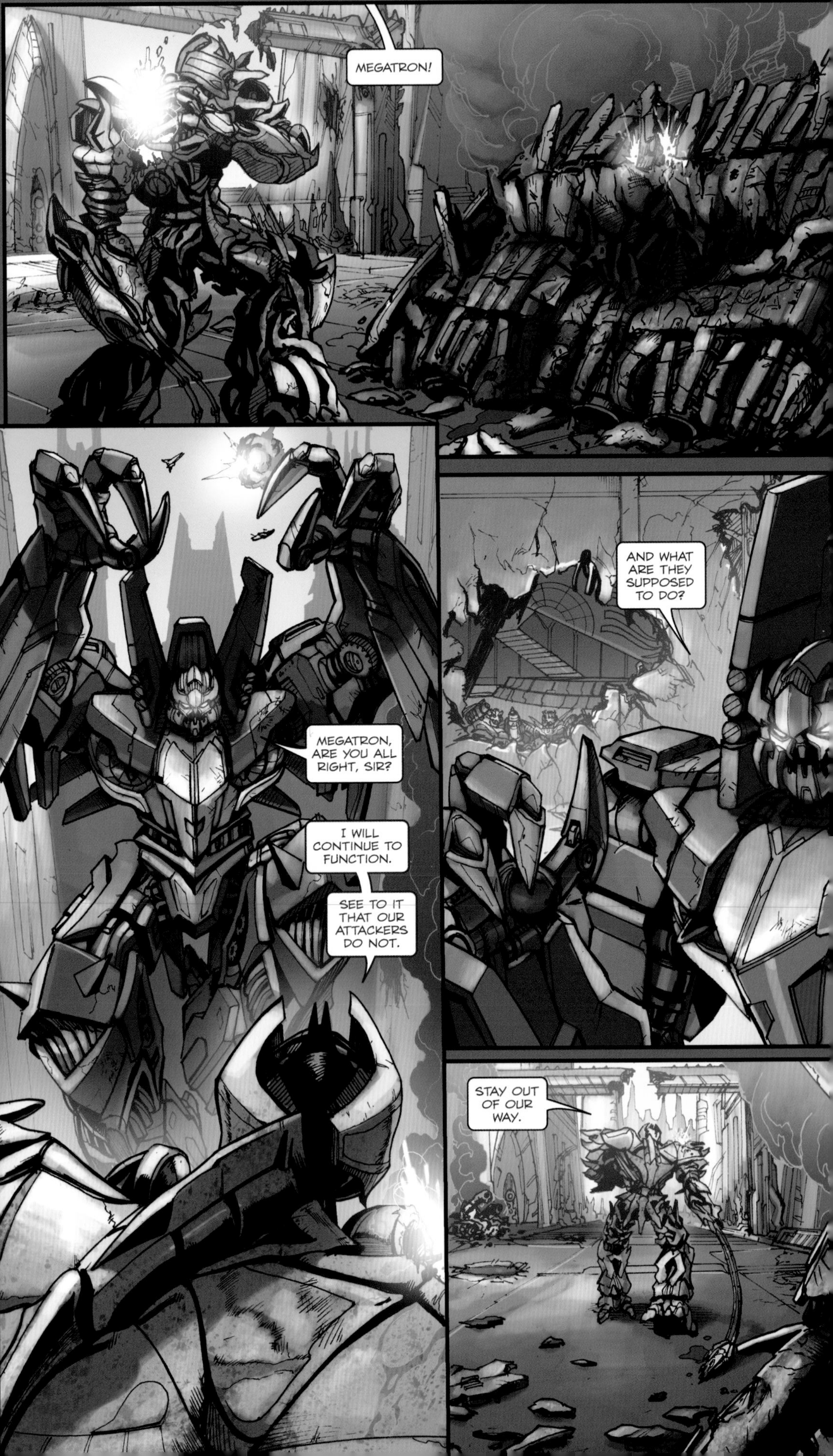
MEGATRON!
MEGATRON, ARE YOU ALL RIGHT, SIR?
I WILL CONTINUE TO FUNCTION.
SEE TO IT THAT OUR ATTACKERS DO NOT.
AND WHAT ARE THEY SUPPOSED TO DO?
STAY OUT OF OUR WAY.

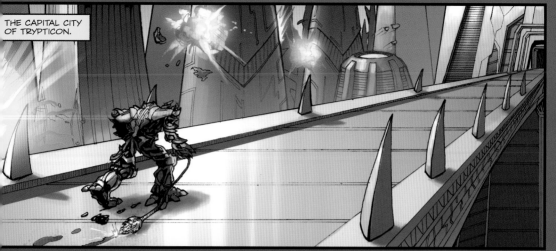

THE CAPITAL CITY OF TRYPTICON.

HOME TO MEGATRON.

THE RELIC WAITS FOR HIM TO RETURN. WAITS FOR MEGATRON TO UNCOVER ITS SECRETS

MEGATRON IS SEVERELY WOUNDED, YET SOMETHING IS CALLING TO HIM. SOMETHING *NEEDS* HIM.

OMETHING IS
IDDEN BENEATH
HE CRUST.

BUT AS MEGATRON BEGINS TO SCRAPE AWAY THE PAST...

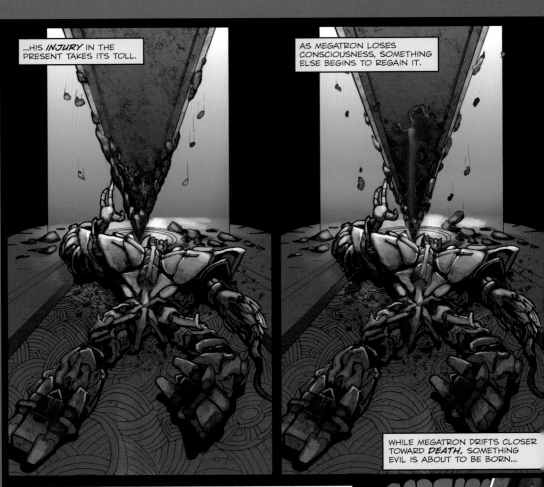

...HIS *INJURY* IN THE PRESENT TAKES ITS TOLL.

AS MEGATRON LOSES CONSCIOUSNESS, SOMETHING ELSE BEGINS TO REGAIN IT.

WHILE MEGATRON DRIFTS CLOSER TOWARD *DEATH,* SOMETHING EVIL IS ABOUT TO BE BORN...

...AGAIN.

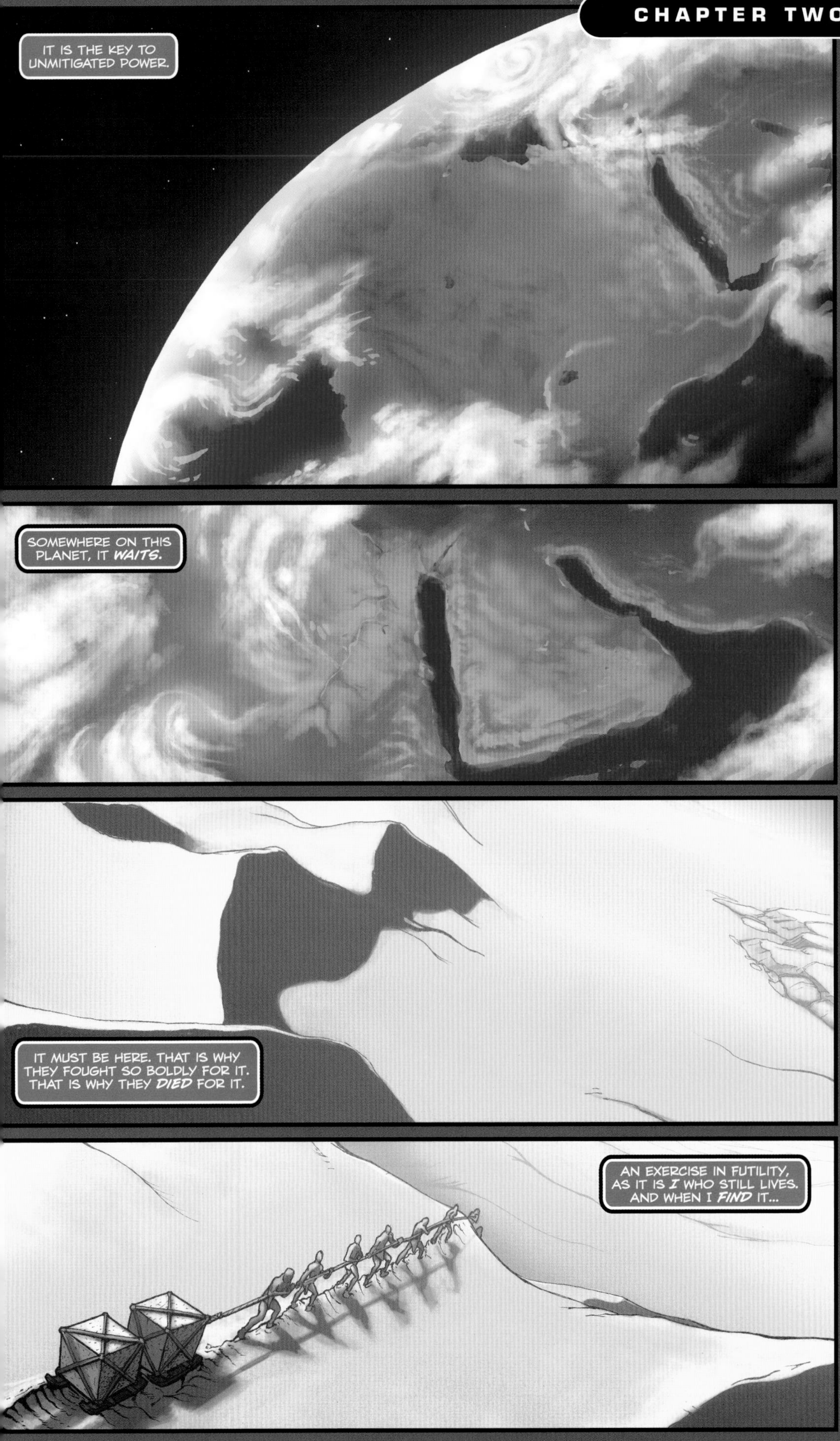
IT IS THE KEY TO UNMITIGATED POWER.
SOMEWHERE ON THIS PLANET, IT *WAITS.*
IT MUST BE HERE. THAT IS WHY THEY FOUGHT SO BOLDLY FOR IT. THAT IS WHY THEY *DIED* FOR IT.
AN EXERCISE IN FUTILITY, AS IT IS *I* WHO STILL LIVES. AND WHEN I *FIND* IT...

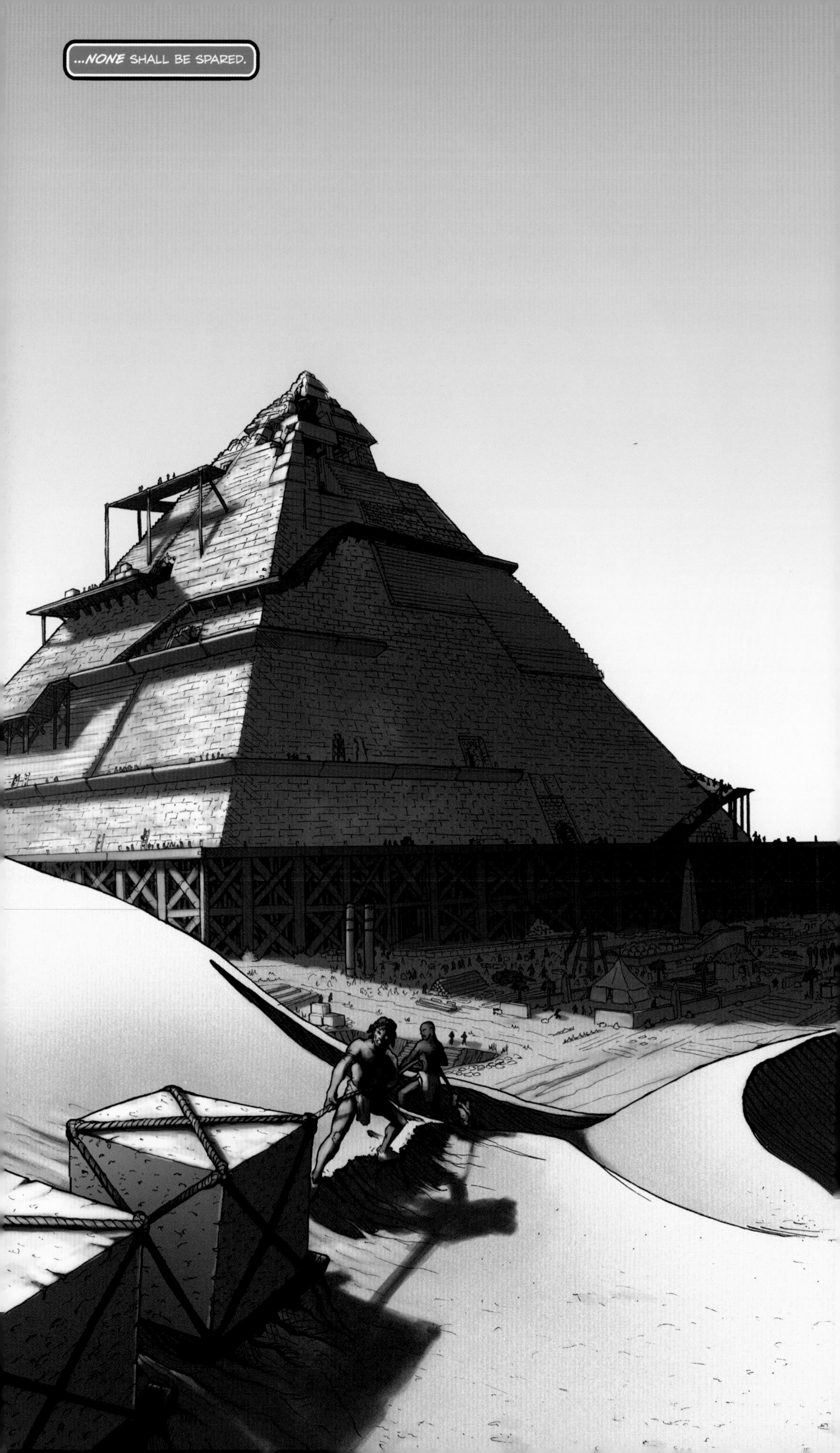
...NONE SHALL BE SPARED.

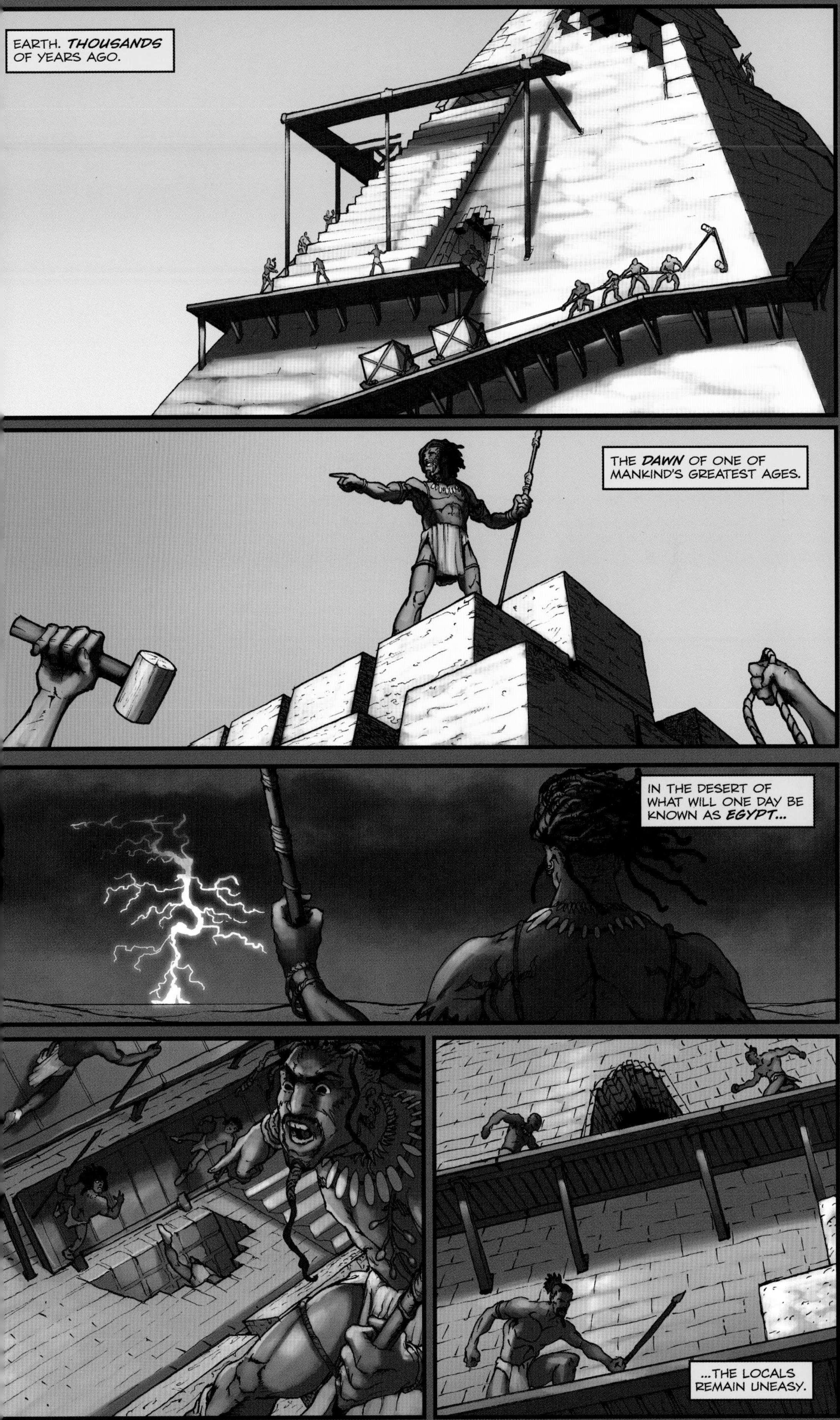
EARTH. *THOUSANDS* OF YEARS AGO.
THE *DAWN* OF ONE OF MANKIND'S GREATEST AGES.
IN THE DESERT OF WHAT WILL ONE DAY BE KNOWN AS *EGYPT*...
...THE LOCALS REMAIN UNEASY.

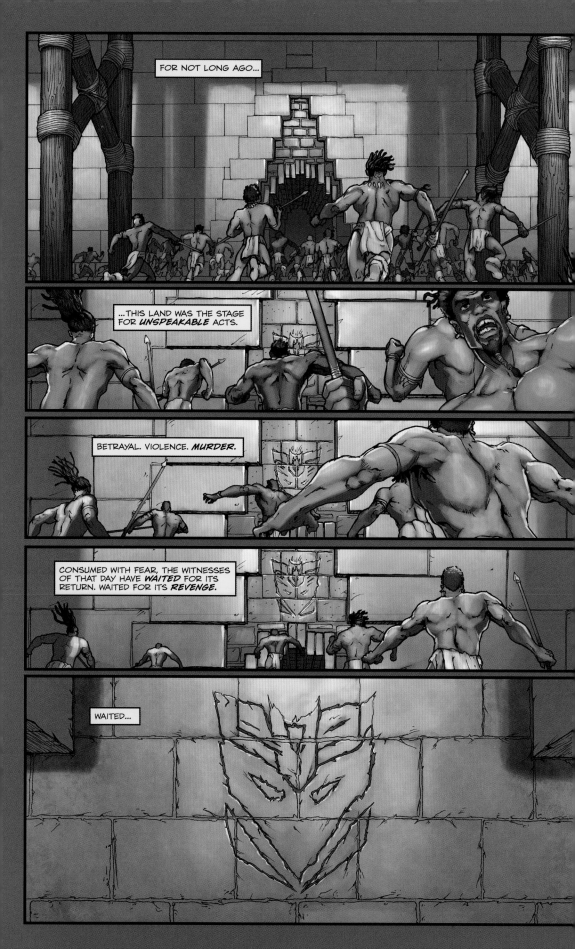

FOR NOT LONG AGO...

...THIS LAND WAS THE STAGE FOR *UNSPEAKABLE* ACTS.

BETRAYAL. VIOLENCE. *MURDER.*

CONSUMED WITH FEAR, THE WITNESSES OF THAT DAY HAVE *WAITED* FOR ITS RETURN. WAITED FOR ITS *REVENGE.*

WAITED...

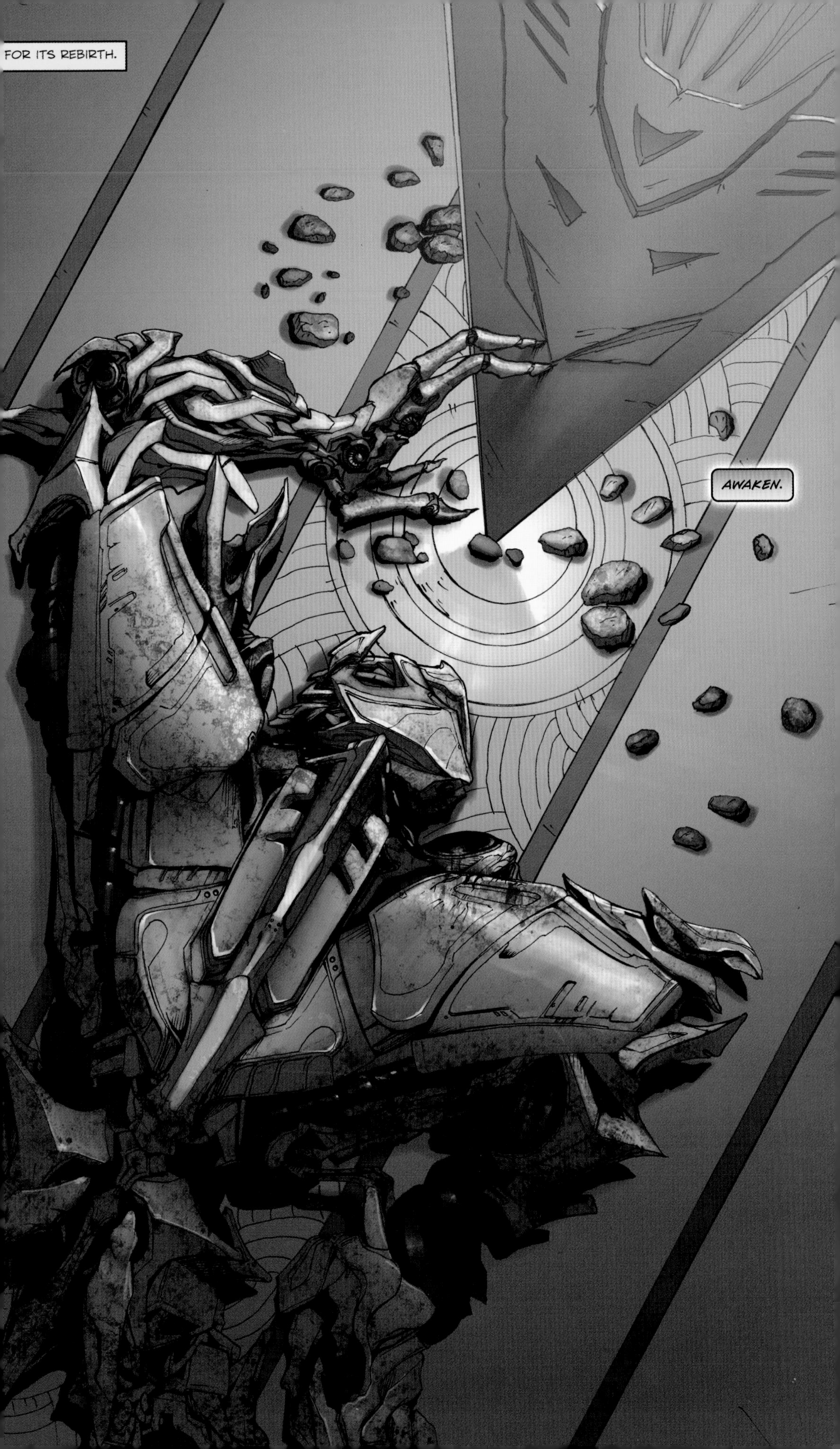
FOR ITS REBIRTH.
AWAKEN.

LATER.

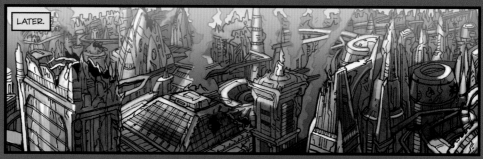

GOT TO KEEP -:HHN:- PUSHING, EVERYONE!

I'M TRYING, *CLOCKER*.

THAT MAKES *EIGHT* IN THIS SECTION ALONE. WHAT HAPPENED?

THIS WAS A SURPRISE ATTACK, BUT BY *WHOM* AND *WHY* REMAIN UNCLEAR.

ANSWERS WILL COME LATER. FIRST, WE MUST TEND TO THE *VICTIMS*.

ALL OF THEM.

THIS CAN'T BE GOOD. NOPE. *NOT* AT ALL. I GET THE FEELING THAT THIS IS THE START OF SOMETHING *BIG*.

HMM. COULD BE, BUT THEN AGAIN, IT'S NOT LIKE WE'RE GOING TO HAVE ANYTHING TO DO WITH A LARGER FIGHT, YOU KNOW? WHAT DO WE DO? WE STAND *GUARD*. THAT'S ABOUT IT.

AND THAT'S *ALL* YOU'RE GOING TO DO, GOT IT? UNLESS YOU WANT TO BE *REPLACED* BY DRONES.

AT EASE, YOU TWO.

DID YOU NOTICE ANYTHING DIFFERENT WITH THE *ALLSPARK* DURING THE FIGHT?

NO, SIR. WE WERE TOO BUSY DODGING BLASTS FROM THAT *TANK* THING.

NOT EVEN WHEN YOU ENGAGED THE "TANK THING"?

NO, SIR. NOTHING AT ALL.

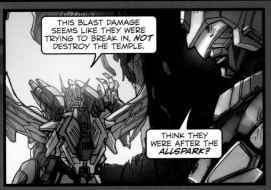

THIS BLAST DAMAGE SEEMS LIKE THEY WERE TRYING TO BREAK IN, *NOT* DESTROY THE TEMPLE.

THINK THEY WERE AFTER THE *ALLSPARK*?

I'D SAY SO. BUT I KNOW SOMEONE WHO MIGHT KNOW *MORE*.

HNN. WH-WHAT HAPPENED?

YOUR WOUND WAS SEVERE, BUT I HAVE USED WHAT LITTLE *STRENGTH* I HAVE TO TREAT IT.

SHOW YOURSELF.

THAT IS... IMPOSSIBLE... WITHOUT YOUR *HELP.*

I AM MEGATRON, *PROTECTOR* OF CYBERTRON. WHAT MAKES YOU THINK THAT I AM ONE TO HELP? SHOW YOURSELF AND FACE YOUR PUNISHM—

BECAUSE I SHALL MAKE YOU *LORD* MEGATRON, *RULER* OF CYBERTRON. BUT FIRST...

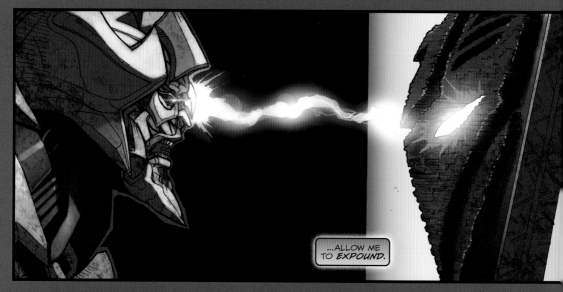

...ALLOW ME TO *EXPOUND.*

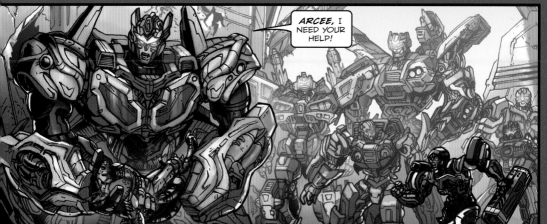

ARCEE, I NEED YOUR HELP!

I'M NOT GETTING ANY KIND OF READINGS, OPTIMUS. THIS ONE'S *GONE*.

I'M SORRY TO HEAR THAT. PERHAPS WE COULD HAVE LEARNED WHAT THEIR *INTENTIONS* WERE.

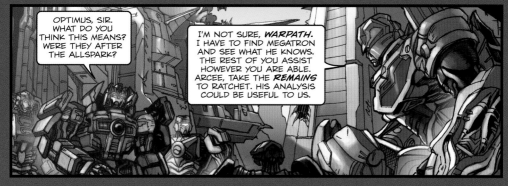

OPTIMUS, SIR. WHAT DO YOU THINK THIS MEANS? WERE THEY AFTER THE ALLSPARK?

I'M NOT SURE, *WARPATH*. I HAVE TO FIND MEGATRON AND SEE WHAT HE KNOWS. THE REST OF YOU ASSIST HOWEVER YOU ARE ABLE. ARCEE, TAKE THE *REMAINS* TO RATCHET. HIS ANALYSIS COULD BE USEFUL TO US.

WANT TO HELP ME WITH THIS ONE, CLOCKER?

YOU GOT IT.

I'LL BE IN TOUCH.

33

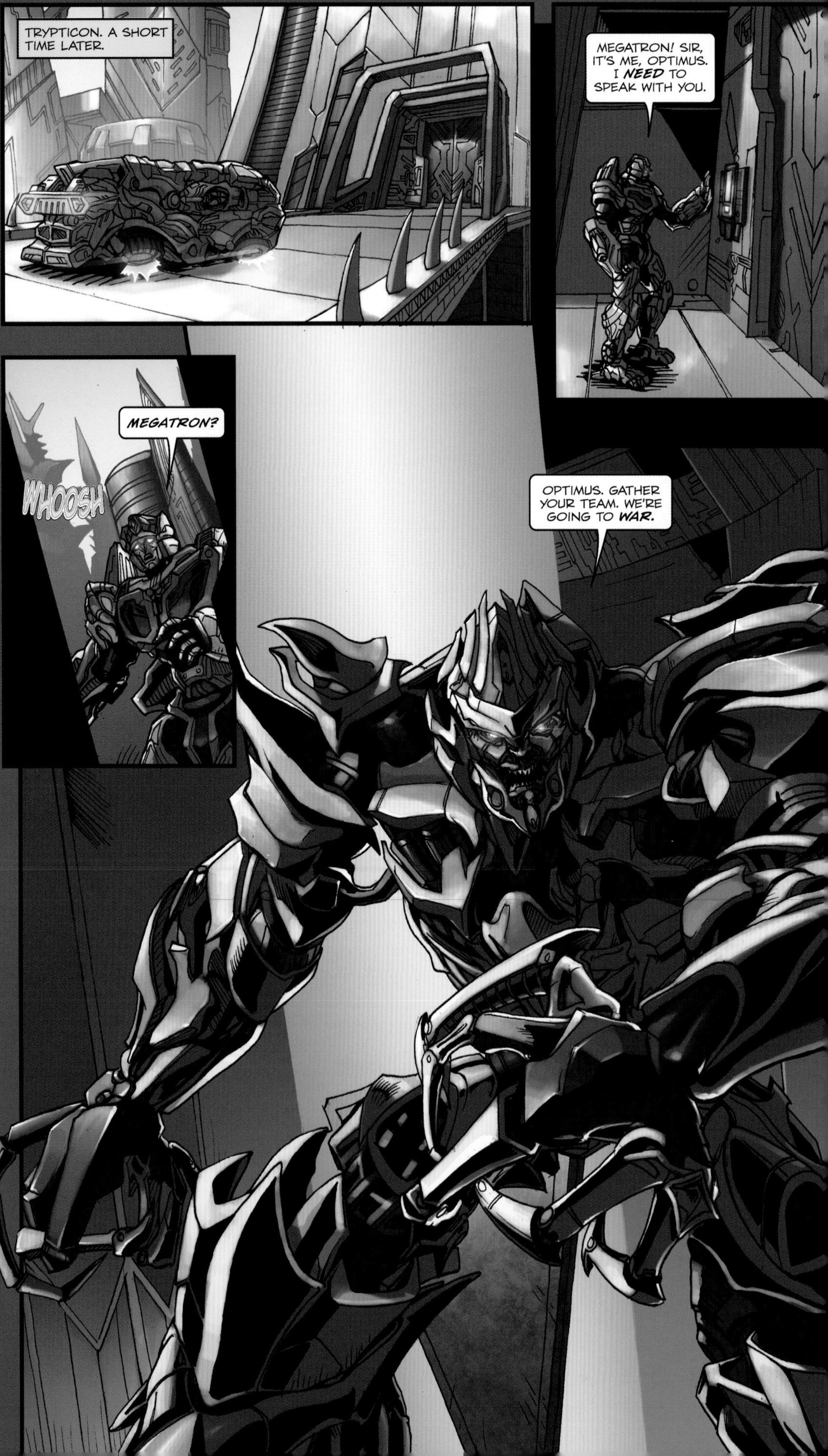
TRYPTICON. A SHORT TIME LATER.
MEGATRON! SIR, IT'S ME, OPTIMUS. I NEED TO SPEAK WITH YOU.
MEGATRON?
WHOOSH
OPTIMUS. GATHER YOUR TEAM. WE'RE GOING TO WAR.

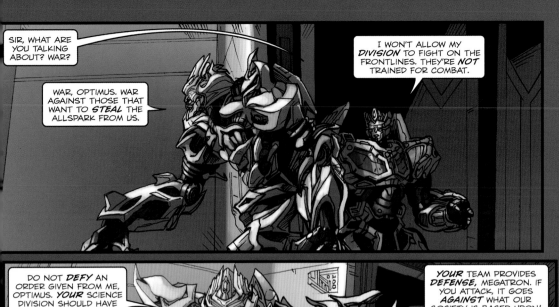

SIR, WHAT ARE YOU TALKING ABOUT? WAR?

WAR, OPTIMUS. WAR AGAINST THOSE THAT WANT TO *STEAL* THE ALLSPARK FROM US.

I WON'T ALLOW MY *DIVISION* TO FIGHT ON THE FRONTLINES. THEY'RE *NOT* TRAINED FOR COMBAT.

DO NOT *DEFY* AN ORDER GIVEN FROM ME, OPTIMUS. *YOUR* SCIENCE DIVISION SHOULD HAVE KNOWN THAT THE ALLSPARK WOULD BE A *TARGET*. GATHER YOUR TEAM... *NOW*.

YOUR TEAM PROVIDES *DEFENSE*, MEGATRON. IF YOU ATTACK, IT GOES *AGAINST* WHAT OUR SOCIETY IS BASED UPON!

HNN.

THEN IT IS TIME THAT OUR SOCIETY CHANGES.

WHAM

GATHER YOUR TEAM, OPTIMUS. I WILL *NOT* TELL YOU ANOTHER TIME.

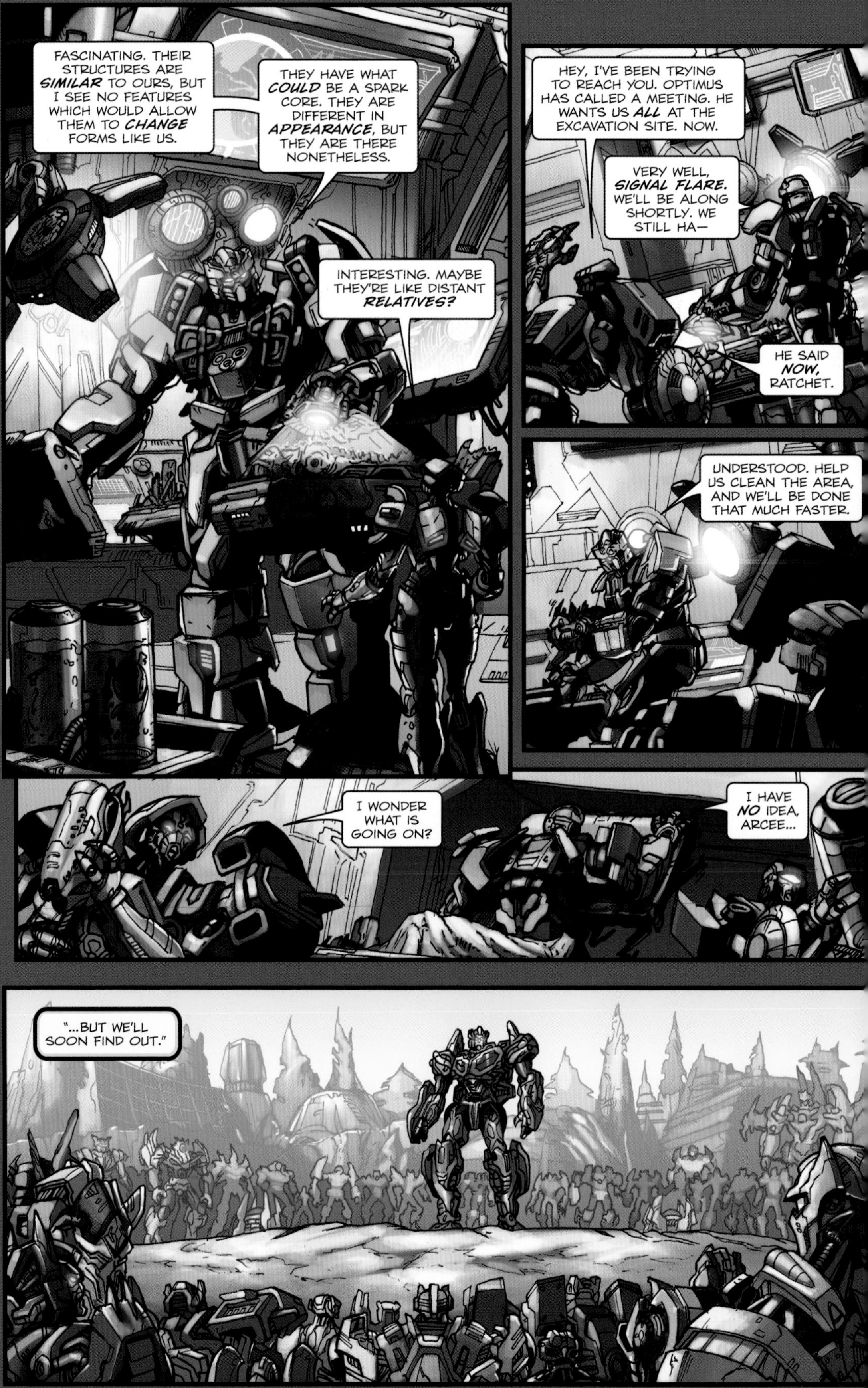
FASCINATING. THEIR STRUCTURES ARE SIMILAR TO OURS, BUT I SEE NO FEATURES WHICH WOULD ALLOW THEM TO CHANGE FORMS LIKE US.
THEY HAVE WHAT COULD BE A SPARK CORE. THEY ARE DIFFERENT IN APPEARANCE, BUT THEY ARE THERE NONETHELESS.
INTERESTING. MAYBE THEY'RE LIKE DISTANT RELATIVES?
HEY, I'VE BEEN TRYING TO REACH YOU. OPTIMUS HAS CALLED A MEETING. HE WANTS US ALL AT THE EXCAVATION SITE. NOW.
VERY WELL, SIGNAL FLARE. WE'LL BE ALONG SHORTLY. WE STILL HA—
HE SAID NOW, RATCHET.
UNDERSTOOD. HELP US CLEAN THE AREA, AND WE'LL BE DONE THAT MUCH FASTER.
I WONDER WHAT IS GOING ON?
I HAVE NO IDEA, ARCEE...
"...BUT WE'LL SOON FIND OUT."

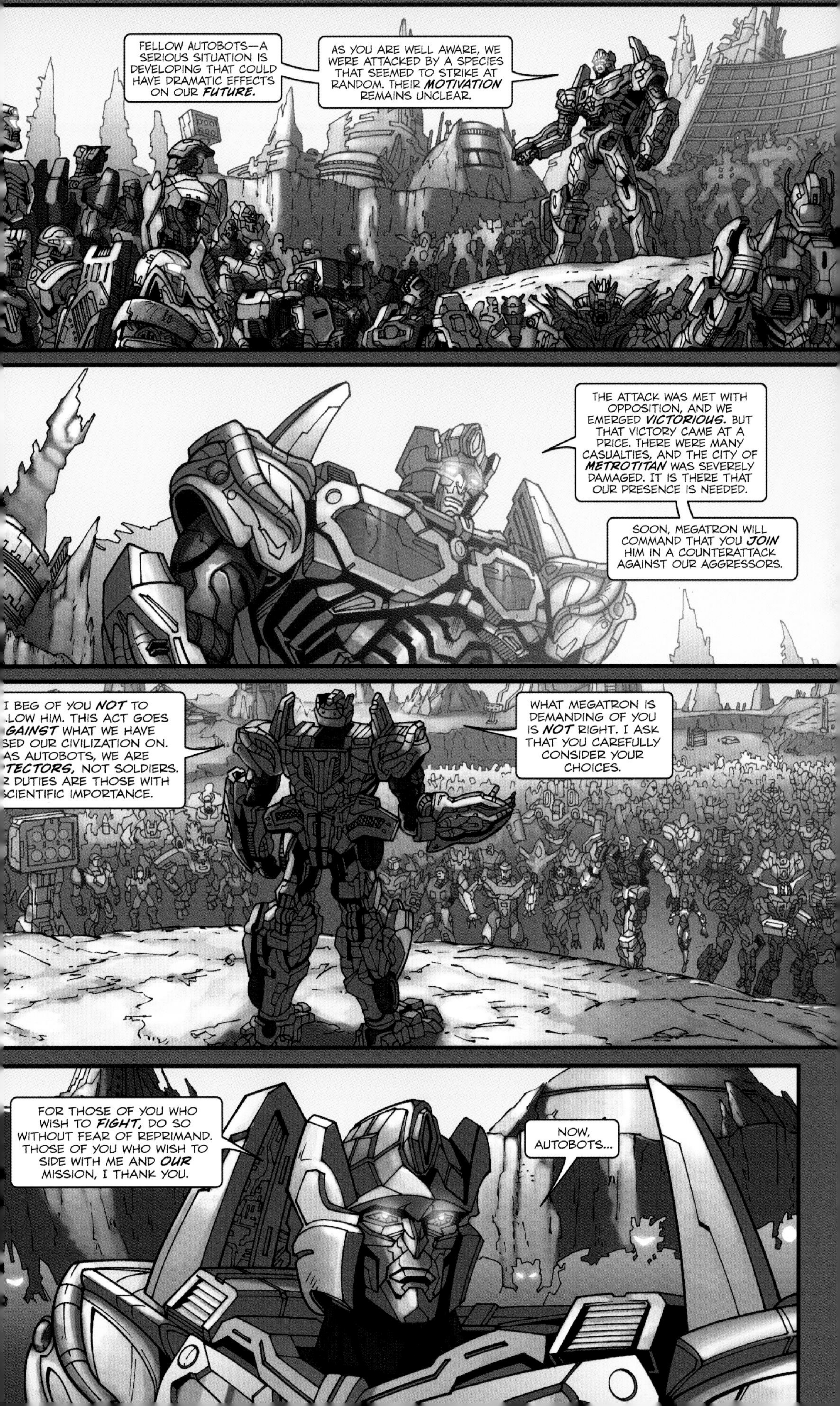
FELLOW AUTOBOTS—A SERIOUS SITUATION IS DEVELOPING THAT COULD HAVE DRAMATIC EFFECTS ON OUR FUTURE.
AS YOU ARE WELL AWARE, WE WERE ATTACKED BY A SPECIES THAT SEEMED TO STRIKE AT RANDOM. THEIR MOTIVATION REMAINS UNCLEAR.
THE ATTACK WAS MET WITH OPPOSITION, AND WE EMERGED VICTORIOUS. BUT THAT VICTORY CAME AT A PRICE. THERE WERE MANY CASUALTIES, AND THE CITY OF METROTITAN WAS SEVERELY DAMAGED. IT IS THERE THAT OUR PRESENCE IS NEEDED.
SOON, MEGATRON WILL COMMAND THAT YOU JOIN HIM IN A COUNTERATTACK AGAINST OUR AGGRESSORS.
I BEG OF YOU NOT TO LOW HIM. THIS ACT GOES GAINST WHAT WE HAVE SED OUR CIVILIZATION ON. AS AUTOBOTS, WE ARE TECTORS, NOT SOLDIERS. DUTIES ARE THOSE WITH SCIENTIFIC IMPORTANCE.
WHAT MEGATRON IS DEMANDING OF YOU IS NOT RIGHT. I ASK THAT YOU CAREFULLY CONSIDER YOUR CHOICES.
FOR THOSE OF YOU WHO WISH TO FIGHT, DO SO WITHOUT FEAR OF REPRIMAND. THOSE OF YOU WHO WISH TO SIDE WITH ME AND OUR MISSION, I THANK YOU.
NOW, AUTOBOTS...

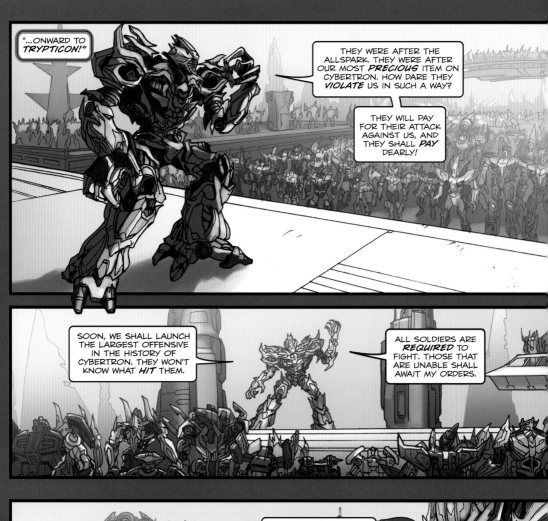

"...ONWARD TO *TRYPTICON!*"

THEY WERE AFTER THE ALLSPARK. THEY WERE AFTER OUR MOST *PRECIOUS* ITEM ON CYBERTRON. HOW DARE THEY *VIOLATE* US IN SUCH A WAY?

THEY WILL PAY FOR THEIR ATTACK AGAINST US, AND THEY SHALL *PAY* DEARLY!

SOON, WE SHALL LAUNCH THE LARGEST OFFENSIVE IN THE HISTORY OF CYBERTRON. THEY WON'T KNOW WHAT *HIT* THEM.

ALL SOLDIERS ARE *REQUIRED* TO FIGHT. THOSE THAT ARE UNABLE SHALL AWAIT MY ORDERS.

UNTIL THIS SITUATION HAS ENDED, *I* AM IN COMMAND. ALL FORCES ON CYBERTRON ANSWER TO *ME*.

THOSE CAPABLE OF *FLIGHT* SHALL INITIATE THE ATTACK. OUR *GROUND* FORCES WILL PICK OFF ANY EVACUEES.

NOW, SOLDIERS... ONWARD TO *VICTORY!*

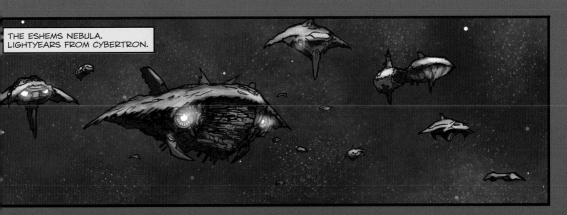

THE ESHEMS NEBULA.
LIGHTYEARS FROM CYBERTRON.

〈CAPTAIN! CAPTAIN! COME LOOK AT THIS!〉

〈WHAT IS IT?〉

〈MULTIPLE TARGETS INCOMING. THEIR *ORIGIN* IS THE ENERGY PLANET!〉

〈THEY'RE MOVING SO FAST!〉

〈SIR! WE'RE UNDER ATTACK!〉

〈DEFEND THE SHIP!〉

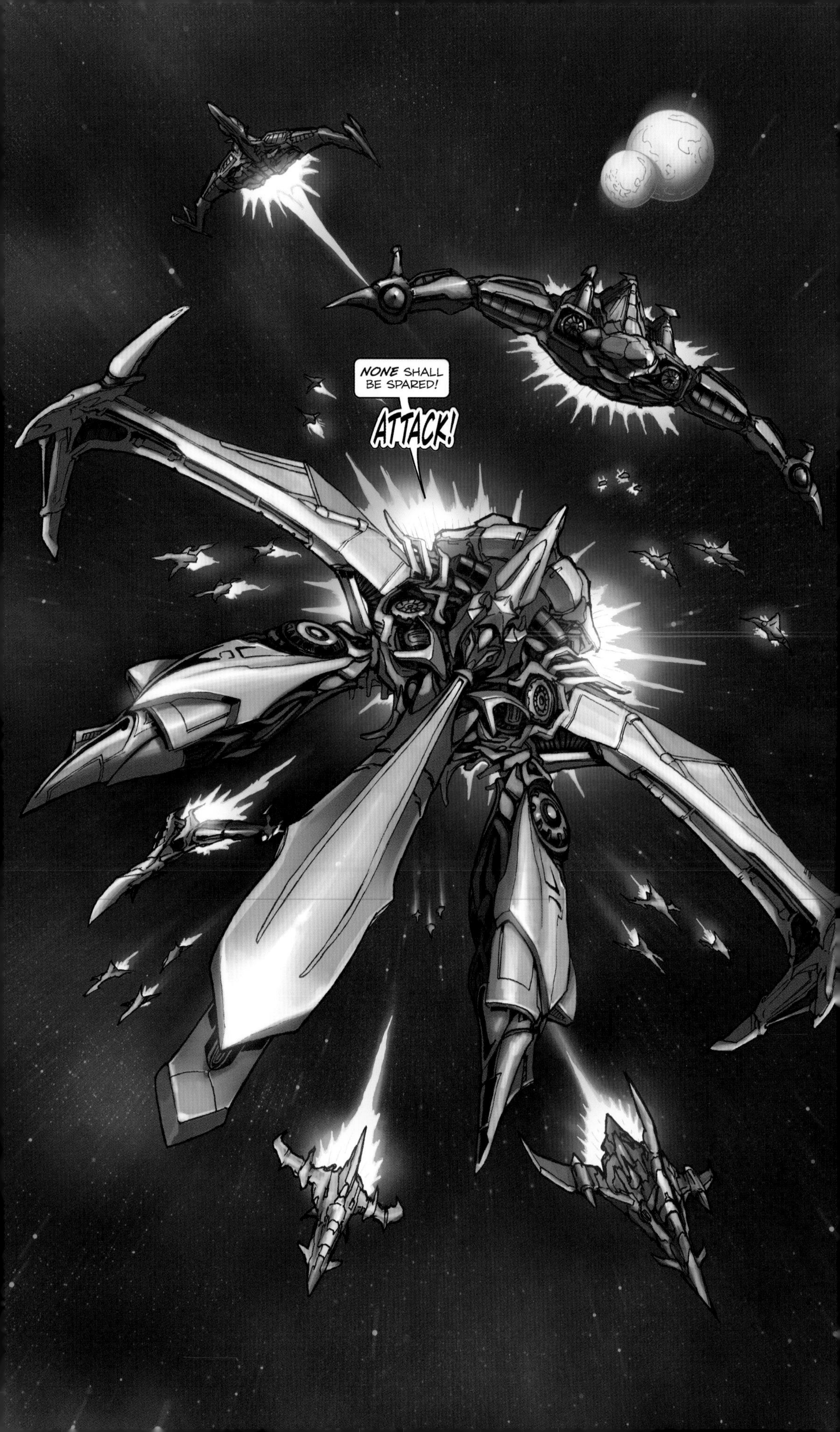
NONE SHALL BE SPARED!
ATTACK!

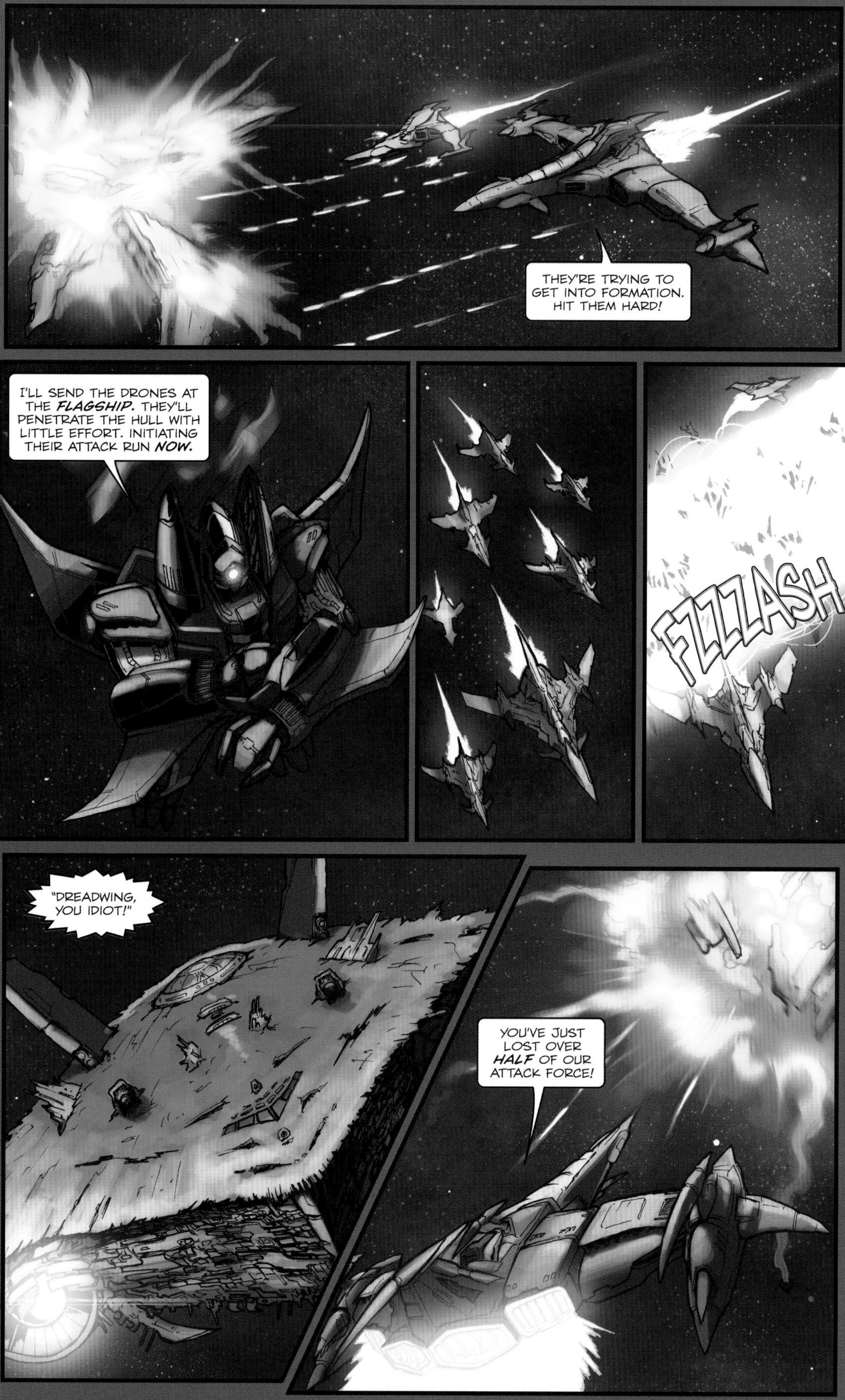
THEY'RE TRYING TO GET INTO FORMATION. HIT THEM HARD!
I'LL SEND THE DRONES AT THE FLAGSHIP. THEY'LL PENETRATE THE HULL WITH LITTLE EFFORT. INITIATING THEIR ATTACK RUN NOW.
FZZZLASH
"DREADWING, YOU IDIOT!"
YOU'VE JUST LOST OVER HALF OF OUR ATTACK FORCE!

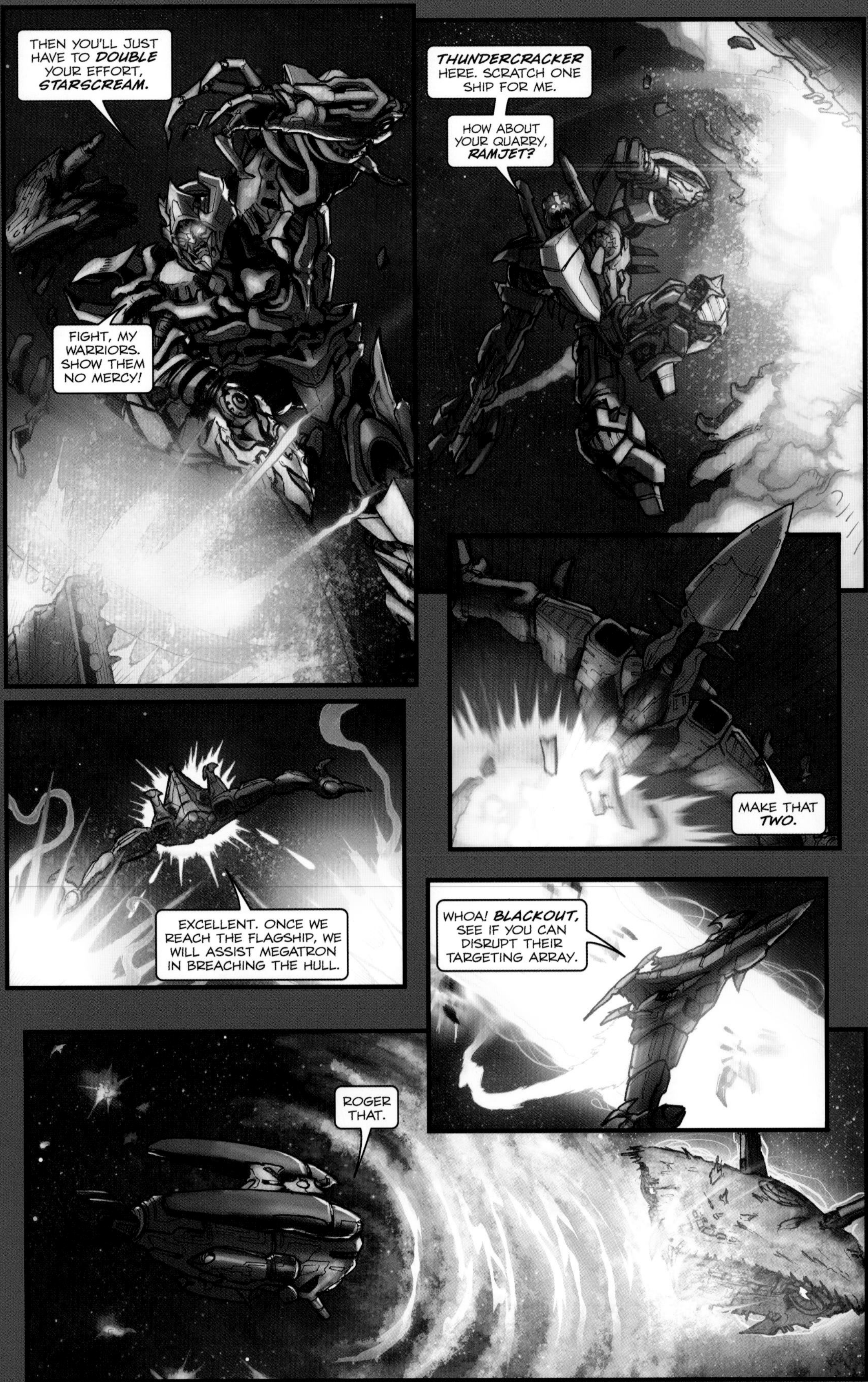
THEN YOU'LL JUST HAVE TO DOUBLE YOUR EFFORT, STARSCREAM.
FIGHT, MY WARRIORS. SHOW THEM NO MERCY!
THUNDERCRACKER HERE. SCRATCH ONE SHIP FOR ME.
HOW ABOUT YOUR QUARRY, RAMJET?
MAKE THAT TWO.
EXCELLENT. ONCE WE REACH THE FLAGSHIP, WE WILL ASSIST MEGATRON IN BREACHING THE HULL.
WHOA! BLACKOUT, SEE IF YOU CAN DISRUPT THEIR TARGETING ARRAY.
ROGER THAT.

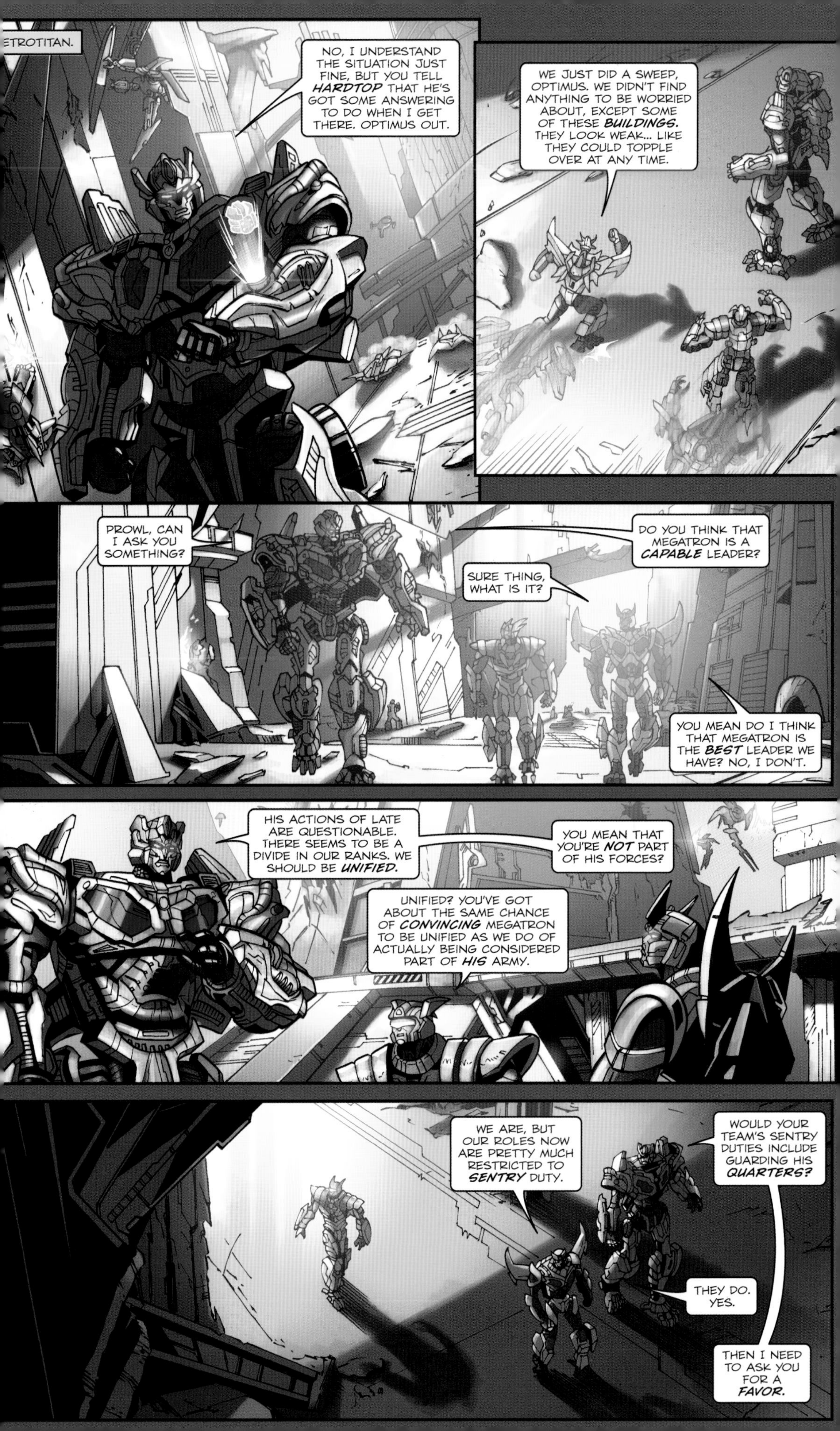

ETROTITAN.
NO, I UNDERSTAND THE SITUATION JUST FINE, BUT YOU TELL HARDTOP THAT HE'S GOT SOME ANSWERING TO DO WHEN I GET THERE. OPTIMUS OUT.
WE JUST DID A SWEEP, OPTIMUS. WE DIDN'T FIND ANYTHING TO BE WORRIED ABOUT, EXCEPT SOME OF THESE BUILDINGS. THEY LOOK WEAK... LIKE THEY COULD TOPPLE OVER AT ANY TIME.
PROWL, CAN I ASK YOU SOMETHING?
SURE THING, WHAT IS IT?
DO YOU THINK THAT MEGATRON IS A CAPABLE LEADER?
YOU MEAN DO I THINK THAT MEGATRON IS THE BEST LEADER WE HAVE? NO, I DON'T.
HIS ACTIONS OF LATE ARE QUESTIONABLE. THERE SEEMS TO BE A DIVIDE IN OUR RANKS. WE SHOULD BE UNIFIED.
YOU MEAN THAT YOU'RE NOT PART OF HIS FORCES?
UNIFIED? YOU'VE GOT ABOUT THE SAME CHANCE OF CONVINCING MEGATRON TO BE UNIFIED AS WE DO OF ACTUALLY BEING CONSIDERED PART OF HIS ARMY.
WE ARE, BUT OUR ROLES NOW ARE PRETTY MUCH RESTRICTED TO SENTRY DUTY.
WOULD YOUR TEAM'S SENTRY DUTIES INCLUDE GUARDING HIS QUARTERS?
THEY DO. YES.
THEN I NEED TO ASK YOU FOR A FAVOR.

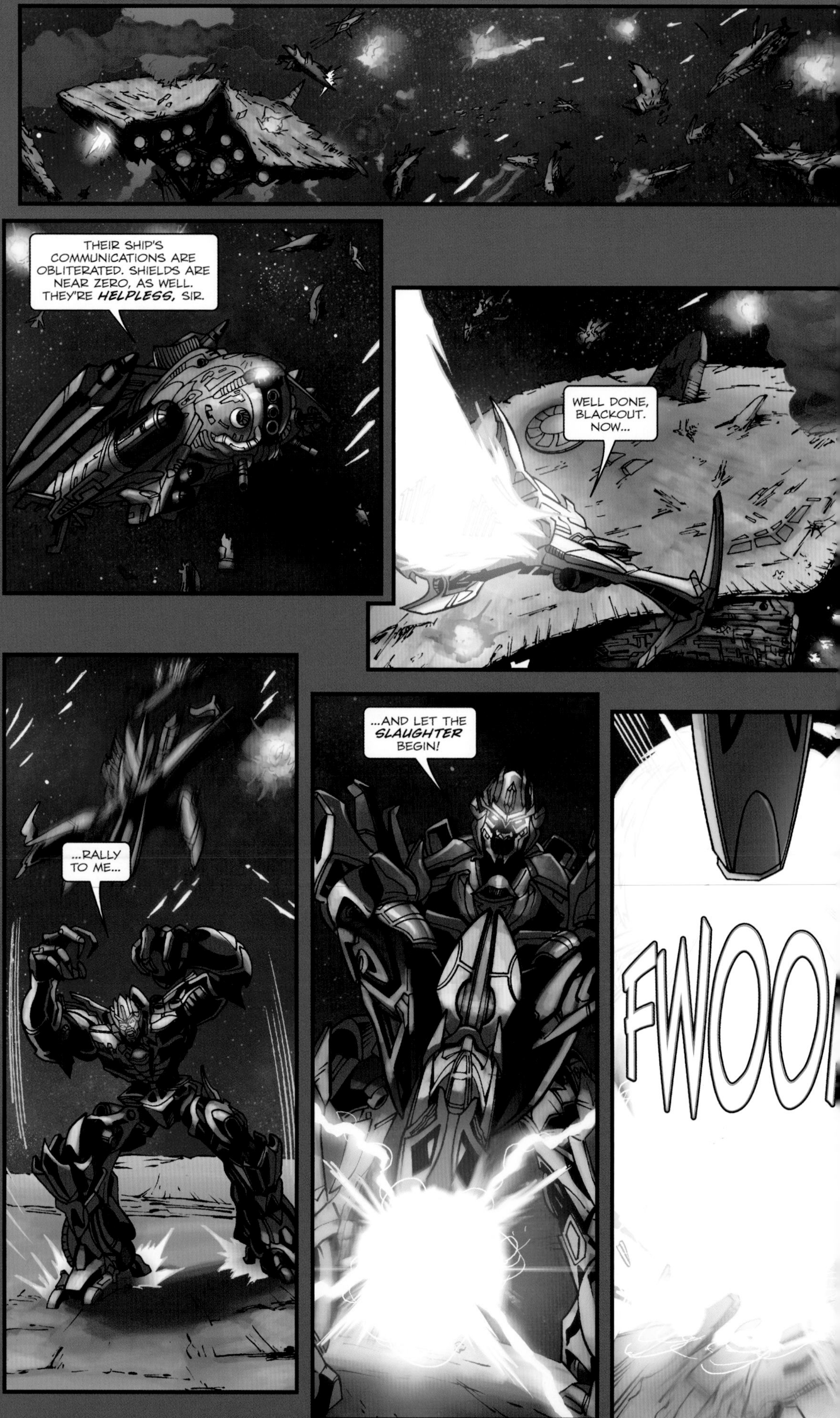
THEIR SHIP'S COMMUNICATIONS ARE OBLITERATED. SHIELDS ARE NEAR ZERO, AS WELL. THEY'RE HELPLESS, SIR.
WELL DONE, BLACKOUT. NOW...
...RALLY TO ME...
...AND LET THE SLAUGHTER BEGIN!
FWOO

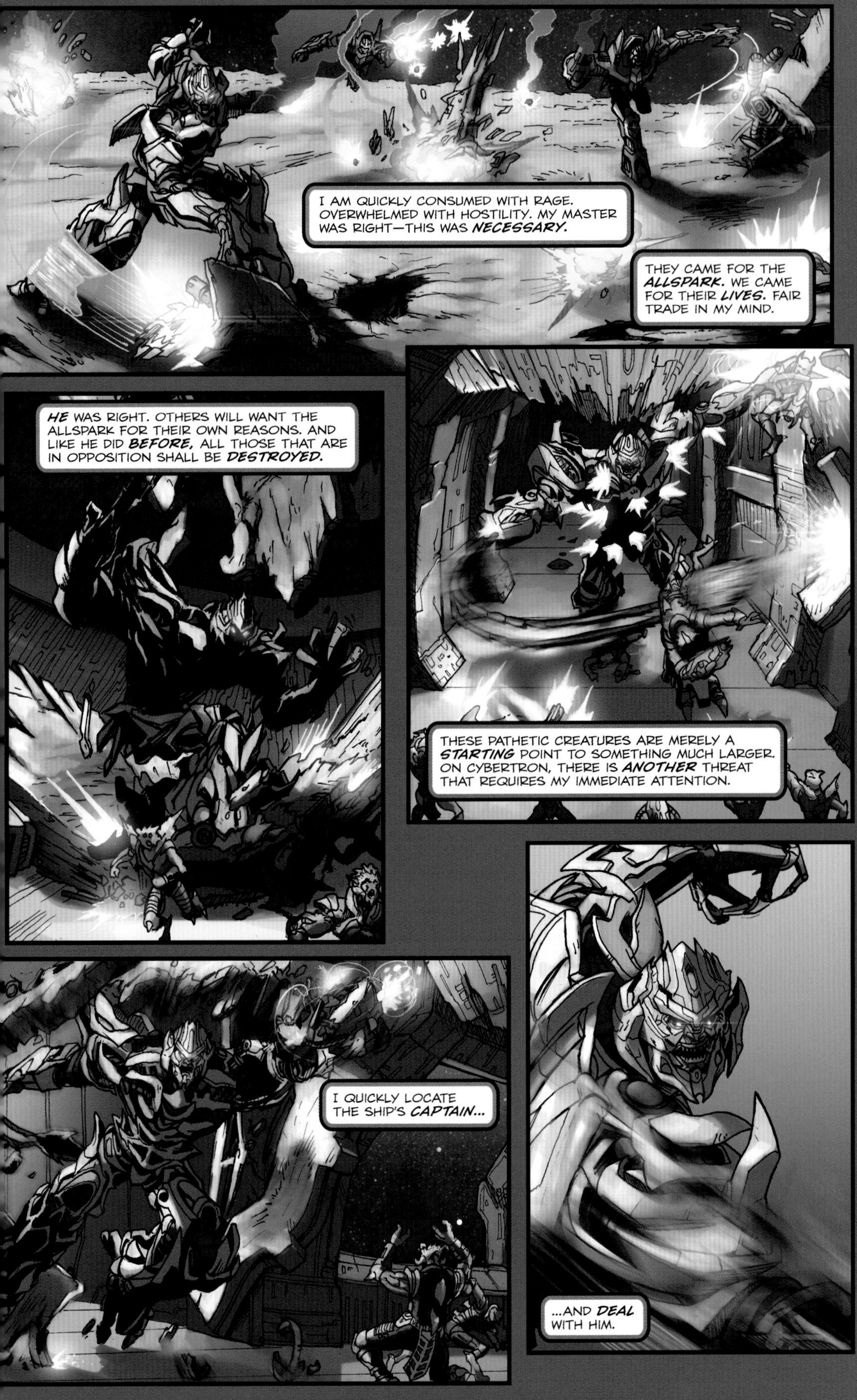
I AM QUICKLY CONSUMED WITH RAGE. OVERWHELMED WITH HOSTILITY. MY MASTER WAS RIGHT—THIS WAS NECESSARY.
THEY CAME FOR THE ALLSPARK. WE CAME FOR THEIR LIVES. FAIR TRADE IN MY MIND.
HE WAS RIGHT. OTHERS WILL WANT THE ALLSPARK FOR THEIR OWN REASONS. AND LIKE HE DID BEFORE, ALL THOSE THAT ARE IN OPPOSITION SHALL BE DESTROYED.
THESE PATHETIC CREATURES ARE MERELY A STARTING POINT TO SOMETHING MUCH LARGER. ON CYBERTRON, THERE IS ANOTHER THREAT THAT REQUIRES MY IMMEDIATE ATTENTION.
I QUICKLY LOCATE THE SHIP'S CAPTAIN...
...AND DEAL WITH HIM.

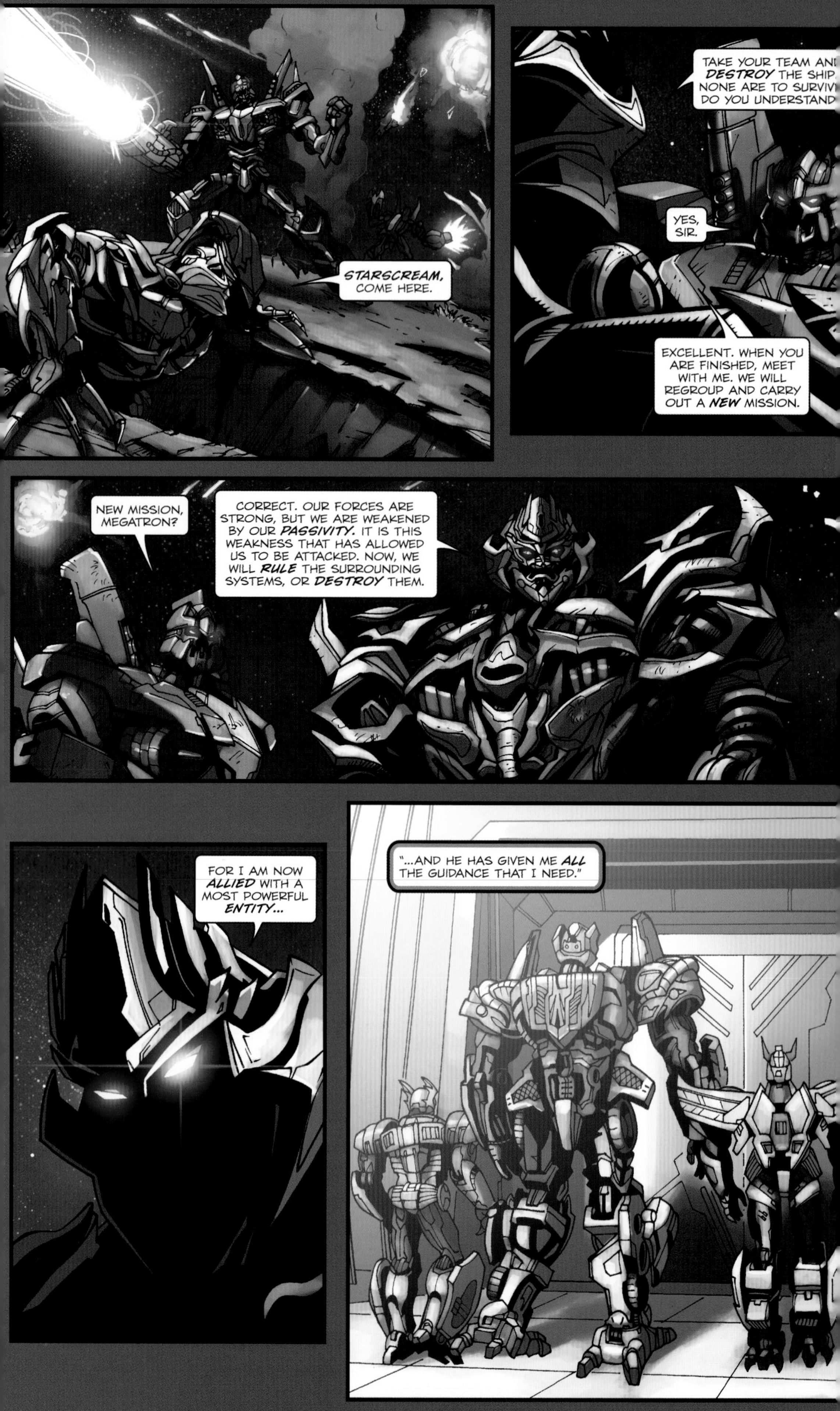
STARSCREAM, COME HERE.
TAKE YOUR TEAM AND DESTROY THE SHIP. NONE ARE TO SURVIVE. DO YOU UNDERSTAND?
YES, SIR.
EXCELLENT. WHEN YOU ARE FINISHED, MEET WITH ME. WE WILL REGROUP AND CARRY OUT A NEW MISSION.
NEW MISSION, MEGATRON?
CORRECT. OUR FORCES ARE STRONG, BUT WE ARE WEAKENED BY OUR PASSIVITY. IT IS THIS WEAKNESS THAT HAS ALLOWED US TO BE ATTACKED. NOW, WE WILL RULE THE SURROUNDING SYSTEMS, OR DESTROY THEM.
FOR I AM NOW ALLIED WITH A MOST POWERFUL ENTITY...
"...AND HE HAS GIVEN ME ALL THE GUIDANCE THAT I NEED."

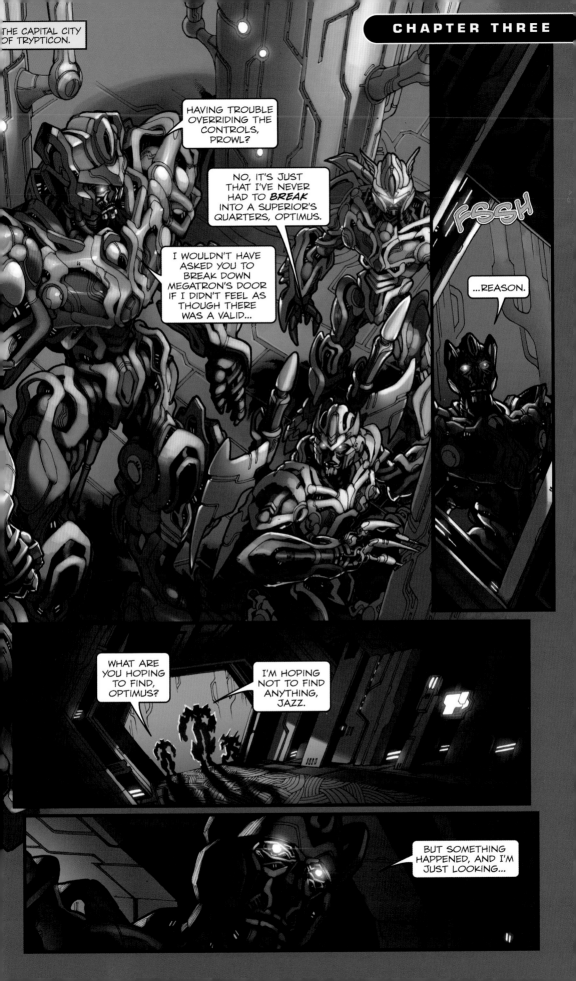

CHAPTER THREE

THE CAPITAL CITY OF TRYPTICON.

HAVING TROUBLE OVERRIDING THE CONTROLS, PROWL?

NO, IT'S JUST THAT I'VE NEVER HAD TO *BREAK* INTO A SUPERIOR'S QUARTERS, OPTIMUS.

I WOULDN'T HAVE ASKED YOU TO BREAK DOWN MEGATRON'S DOOR IF I DIDN'T FEEL AS THOUGH THERE WAS A VALID...

FSSH

...REASON.

WHAT ARE YOU HOPING TO FIND, OPTIMUS?

I'M HOPING NOT TO FIND ANYTHING, JAZZ.

BUT SOMETHING HAPPENED, AND I'M JUST LOOKING...

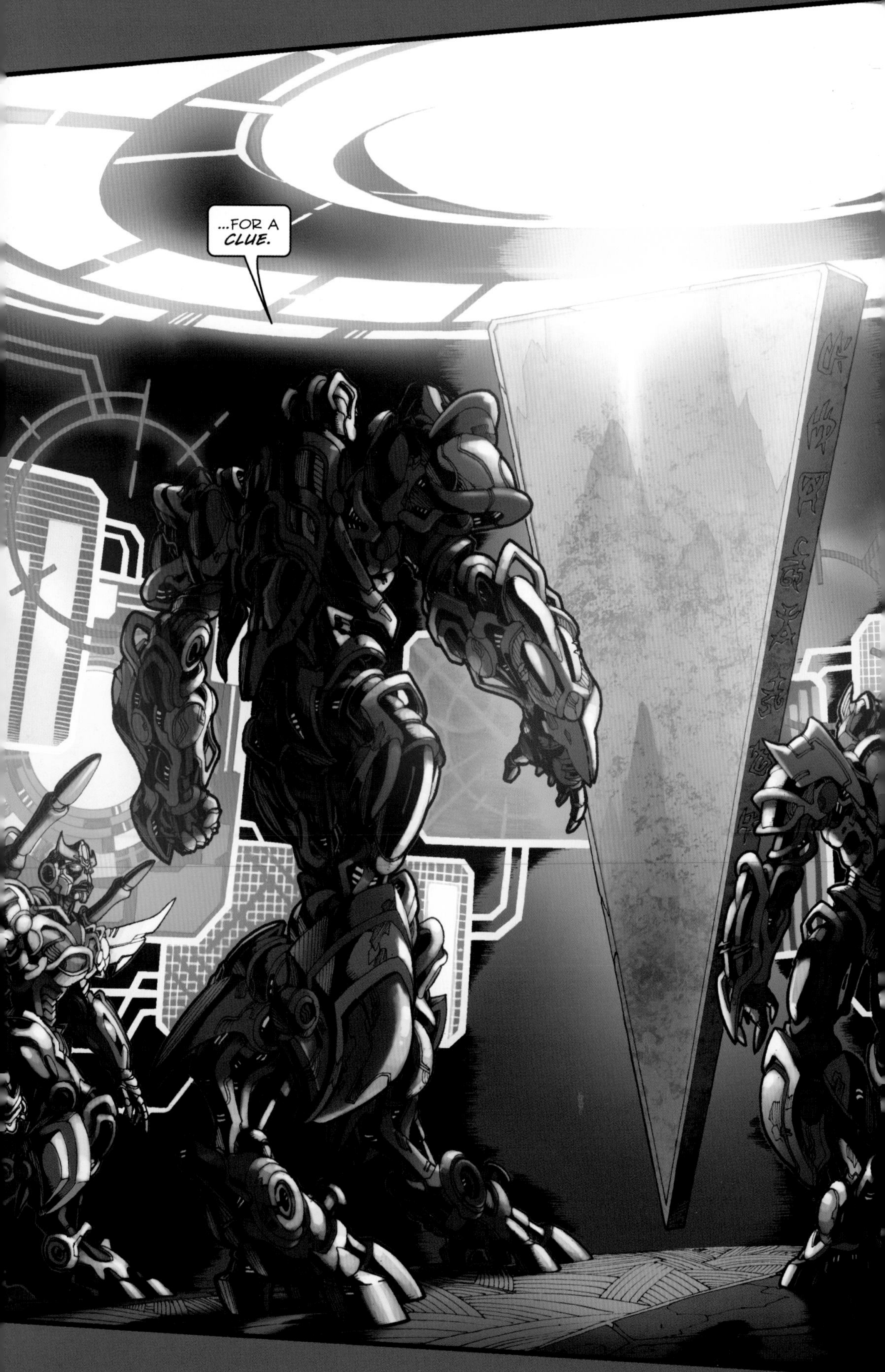
...FOR A CLUE.

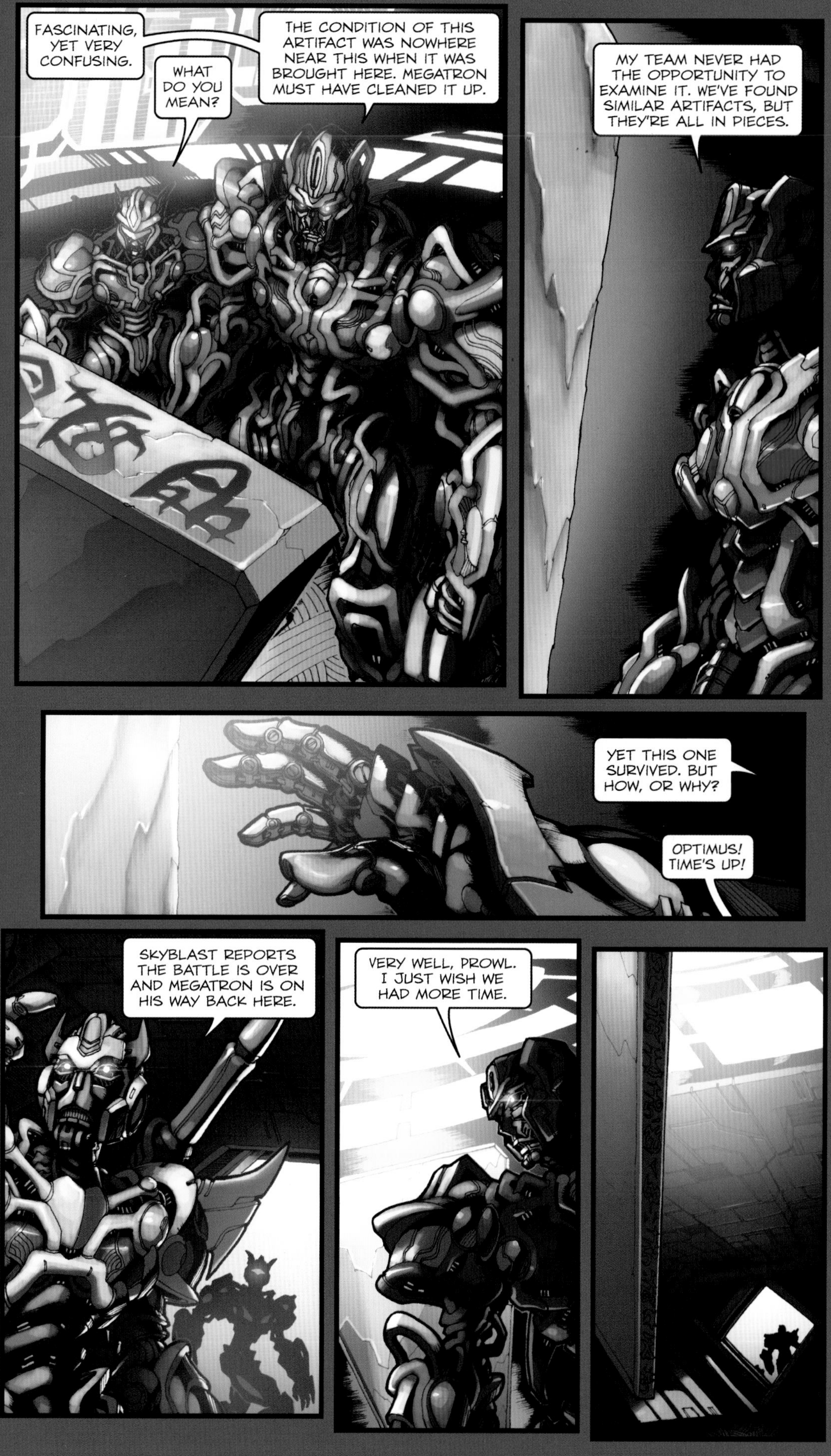
FASCINATING, YET VERY CONFUSING.
WHAT DO YOU MEAN?
THE CONDITION OF THIS ARTIFACT WAS NOWHERE NEAR THIS WHEN IT WAS BROUGHT HERE. MEGATRON MUST HAVE CLEANED IT UP.
MY TEAM NEVER HAD THE OPPORTUNITY TO EXAMINE IT. WE'VE FOUND SIMILAR ARTIFACTS, BUT THEY'RE ALL IN PIECES.
YET THIS ONE SURVIVED. BUT HOW, OR WHY?
OPTIMUS! TIME'S UP!
SKYBLAST REPORTS THE BATTLE IS OVER AND MEGATRON IS ON HIS WAY BACK HERE.
VERY WELL, PROWL. I JUST WISH WE HAD MORE TIME.

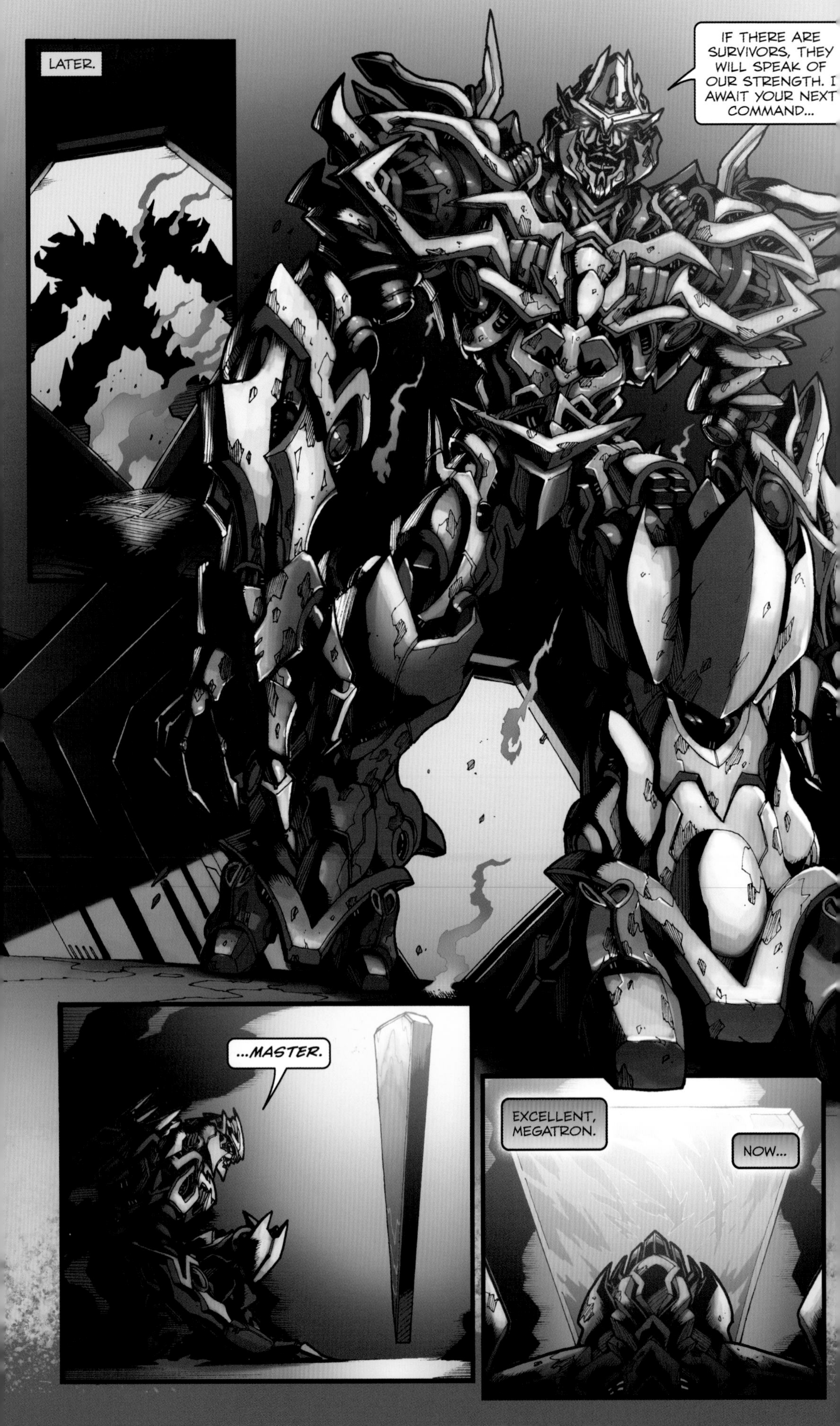
LATER.
IF THERE ARE SURVIVORS, THEY WILL SPEAK OF OUR STRENGTH. I AWAIT YOUR NEXT COMMAND...
...MASTER.
EXCELLENT, MEGATRON.
NOW...

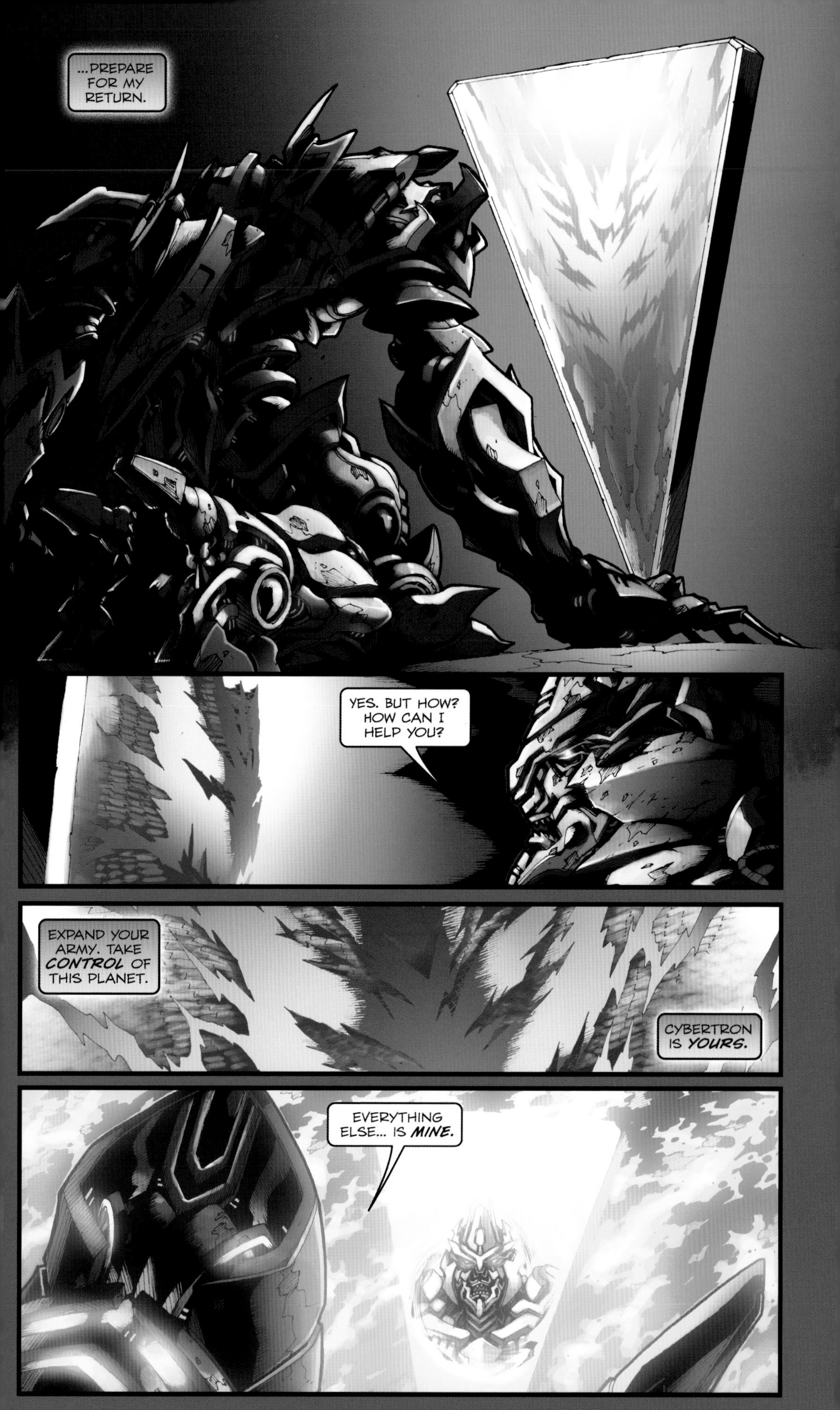
...PREPARE FOR MY RETURN.
YES. BUT HOW? HOW CAN I HELP YOU?
EXPAND YOUR ARMY. TAKE CONTROL OF THIS PLANET.
CYBERTRON IS YOURS.
EVERYTHING ELSE... IS MINE.

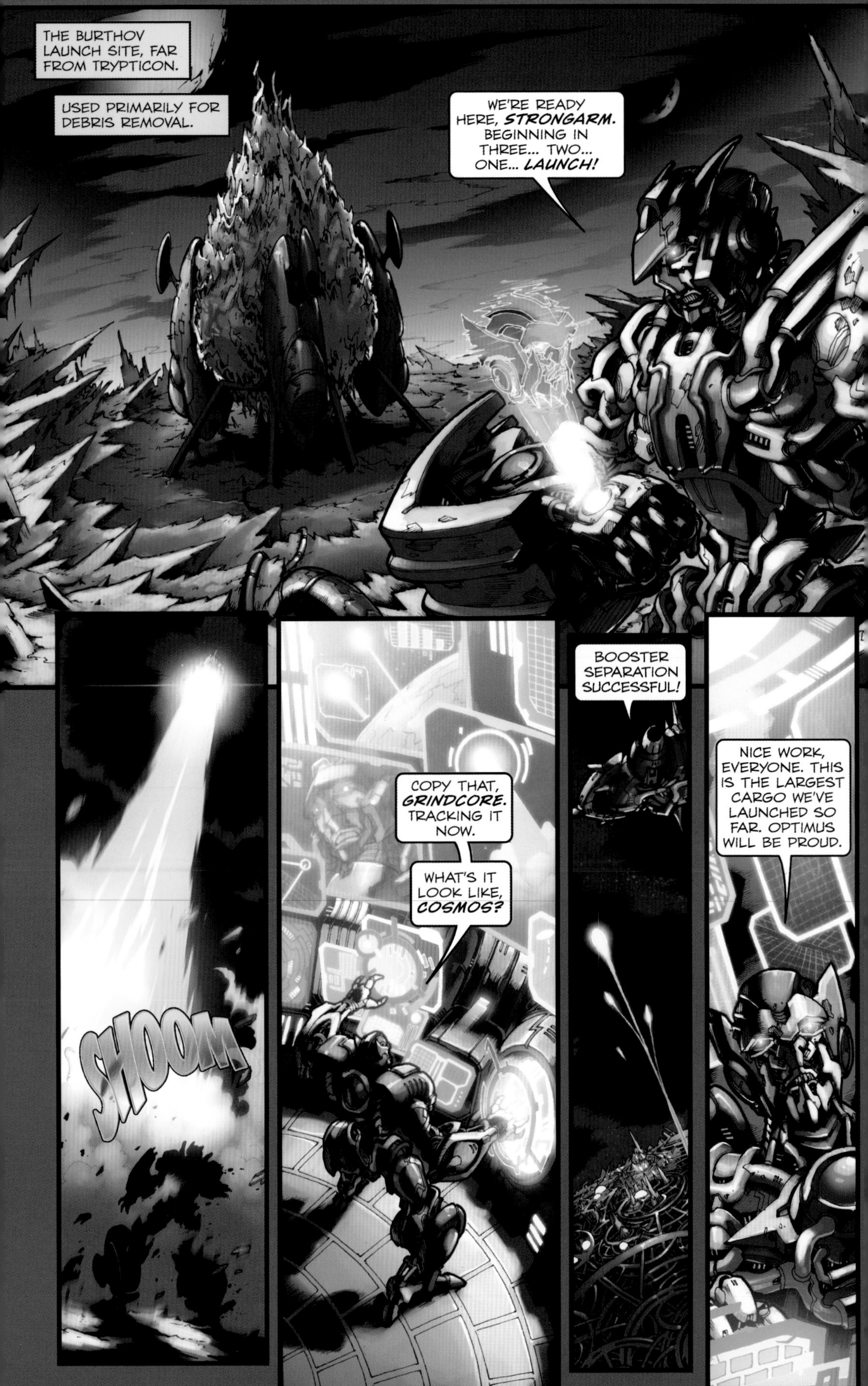
THE BURTHOV LAUNCH SITE, FAR FROM TRYPTICON.
USED PRIMARILY FOR DEBRIS REMOVAL.
WE'RE READY HERE, STRONGARM. BEGINNING IN THREE... TWO... ONE... LAUNCH!
SHOOM
COPY THAT, GRINDCORE. TRACKING IT NOW.
WHAT'S IT LOOK LIKE, COSMOS?
BOOSTER SEPARATION SUCCESSFUL!
NICE WORK, EVERYONE. THIS IS THE LARGEST CARGO WE'VE LAUNCHED SO FAR. OPTIMUS WILL BE PROUD.

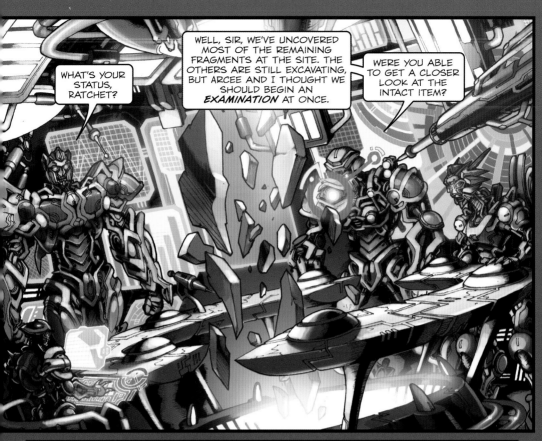

WHAT'S YOUR STATUS, RATCHET?

WELL, SIR, WE'VE UNCOVERED MOST OF THE REMAINING FRAGMENTS AT THE SITE. THE OTHERS ARE STILL EXCAVATING, BUT ARCEE AND I THOUGHT WE SHOULD BEGIN AN *EXAMINATION* AT ONCE.

WERE YOU ABLE TO GET A CLOSER LOOK AT THE INTACT ITEM?

ITS CONDITION WAS *BETTER* THAN WHEN IT WAS DELIVERED.

THAT'S NICE.

MY APOLOGIES, SIR. YOU SAID IT WAS "BETTER"?

IT LOOKED *NEW*.

I THINK I'VE GOT SOMETHING!

WHAT IS IT, *ARCEE?*

I'VE GOT A MATCH. I MEAN, THE PIECES ARE ALL DIFFERENT, BUT THEY ALL SHARE THE *SAME* SYMBOL IN THE SAME AREA.

WHICH SYMBOL?

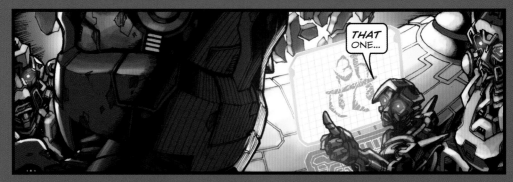

THAT ONE...

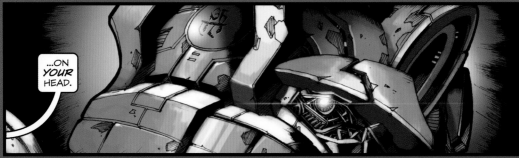

...ON *YOUR* HEAD.

OPTIMUS, THIS IS PROOF THAT THE *DYNASTY OF PRIMES* IS REAL!

AND AS HARD AS IT MAY BE TO ACCEPT, YOU'RE SOMEHOW *CONNECTED*...

"CONNECTED"? YOU MEAN I MIGHT BE...

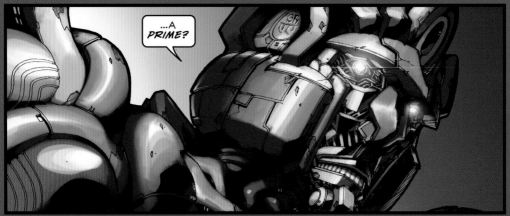

...A *PRIME?*

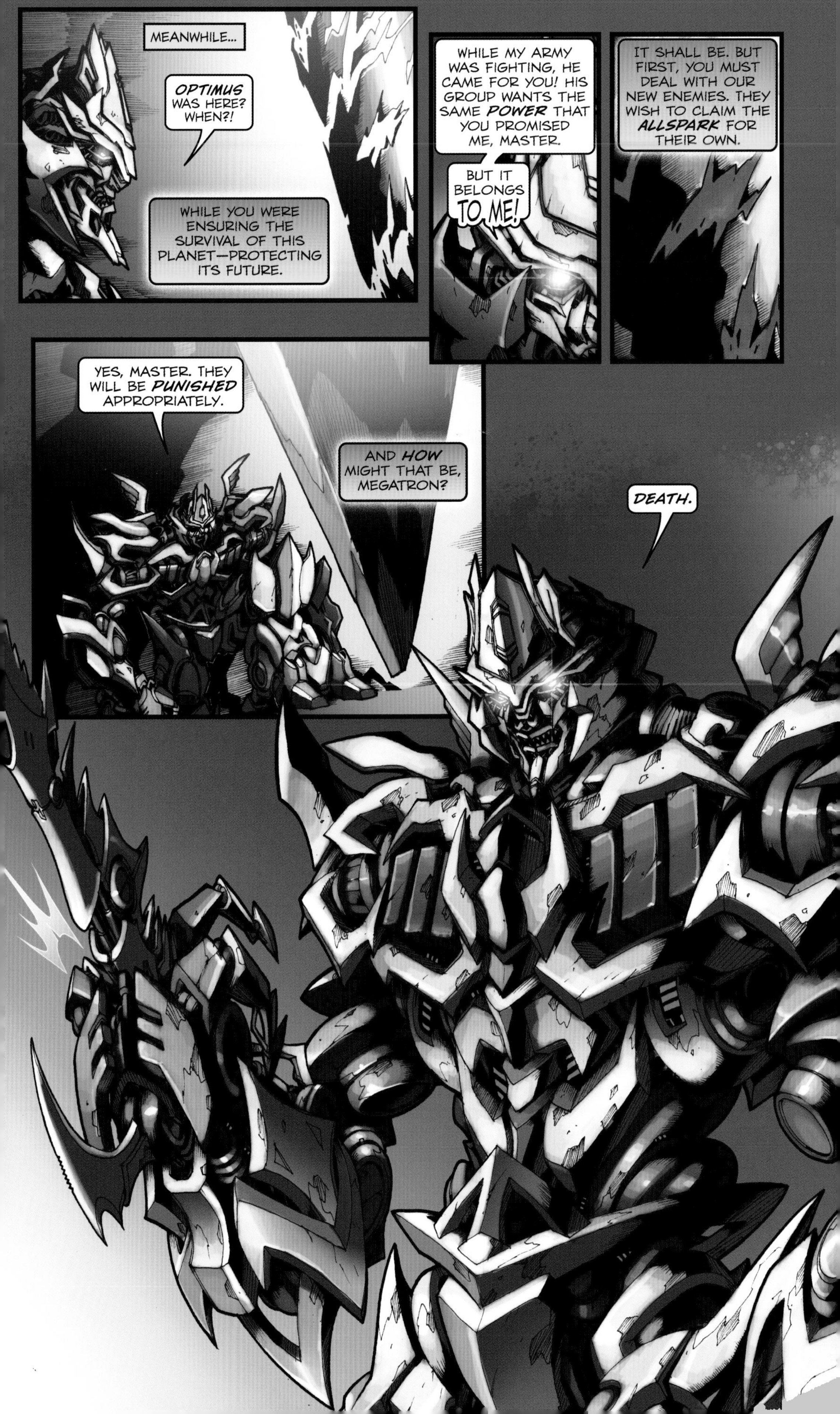
MEANWHILE...
OPTIMUS WAS HERE? WHEN?!
WHILE YOU WERE ENSURING THE SURVIVAL OF THIS PLANET—PROTECTING ITS FUTURE.
WHILE MY ARMY WAS FIGHTING, HE CAME FOR YOU! HIS GROUP WANTS THE SAME POWER THAT YOU PROMISED ME, MASTER.
BUT IT BELONGS TO ME!
IT SHALL BE. BUT FIRST, YOU MUST DEAL WITH OUR NEW ENEMIES. THEY WISH TO CLAIM THE ALLSPARK FOR THEIR OWN.
YES, MASTER. THEY WILL BE PUNISHED APPROPRIATELY.
AND HOW MIGHT THAT BE, MEGATRON?
DEATH.

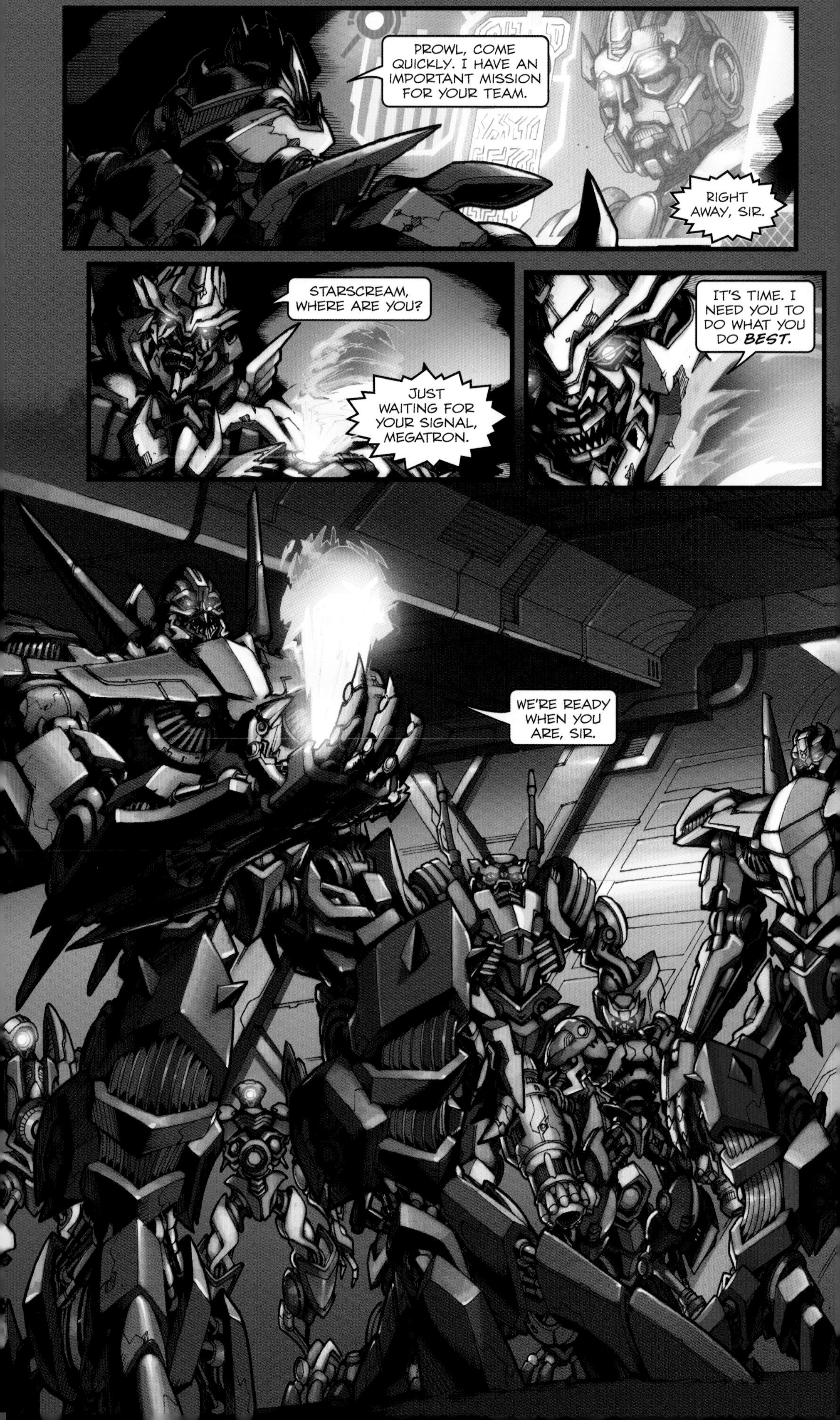
PROWL, COME QUICKLY. I HAVE AN IMPORTANT MISSION FOR YOUR TEAM.
RIGHT AWAY, SIR.
STARSCREAM, WHERE ARE YOU?
JUST WAITING FOR YOUR SIGNAL, MEGATRON.
IT'S TIME. I NEED YOU TO DO WHAT YOU DO **BEST.**
WE'RE READY WHEN YOU ARE, SIR.

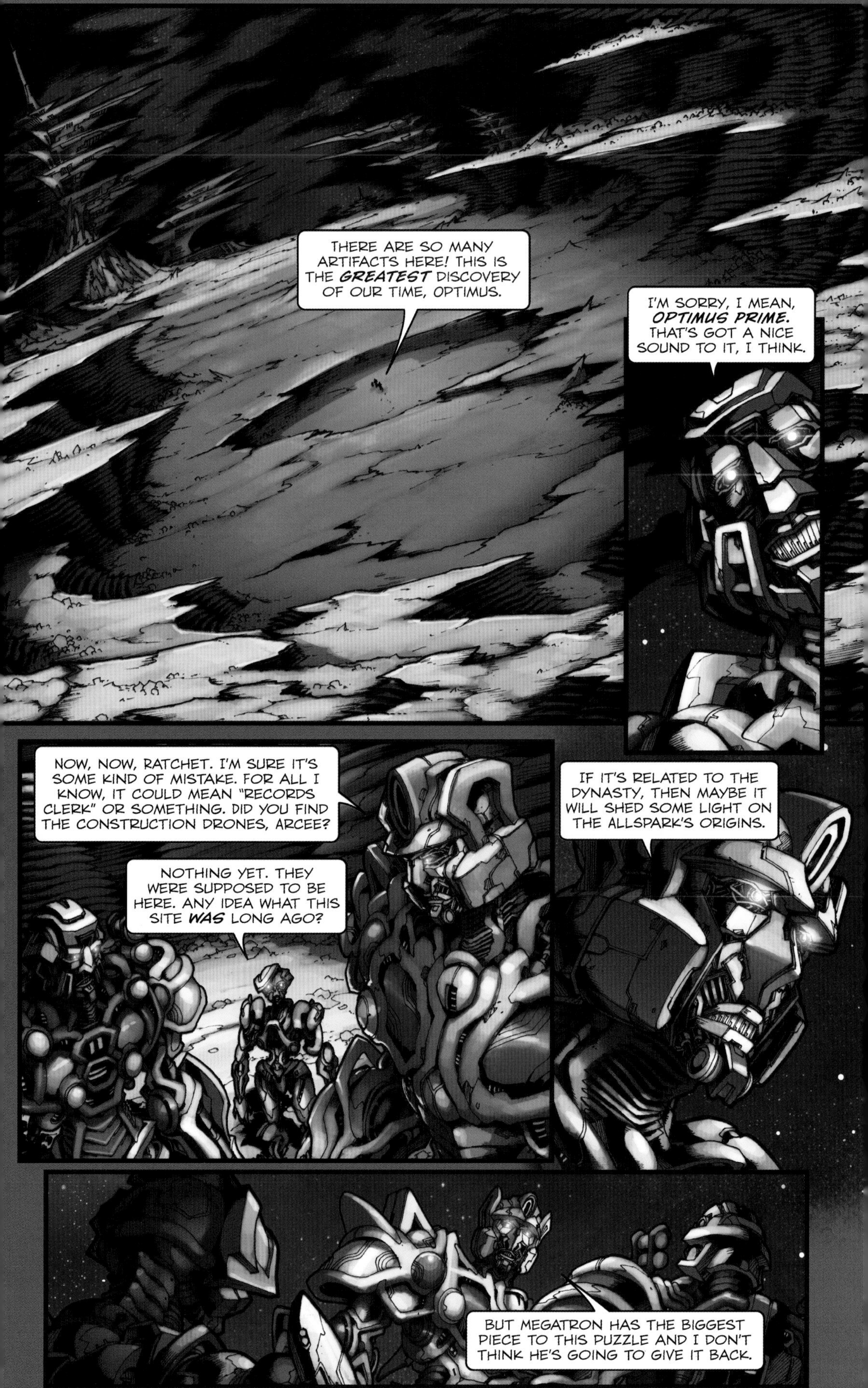
THERE ARE SO MANY ARTIFACTS HERE! THIS IS THE GREATEST DISCOVERY OF OUR TIME, OPTIMUS.
I'M SORRY, I MEAN, OPTIMUS PRIME. THAT'S GOT A NICE SOUND TO IT, I THINK.
NOW, NOW, RATCHET. I'M SURE IT'S SOME KIND OF MISTAKE. FOR ALL I KNOW, IT COULD MEAN "RECORDS CLERK" OR SOMETHING. DID YOU FIND THE CONSTRUCTION DRONES, ARCEE?
NOTHING YET. THEY WERE SUPPOSED TO BE HERE. ANY IDEA WHAT THIS SITE WAS LONG AGO?
IF IT'S RELATED TO THE DYNASTY, THEN MAYBE IT WILL SHED SOME LIGHT ON THE ALLSPARK'S ORIGINS.
BUT MEGATRON HAS THE BIGGEST PIECE TO THIS PUZZLE AND I DON'T THINK HE'S GOING TO GIVE IT BACK.

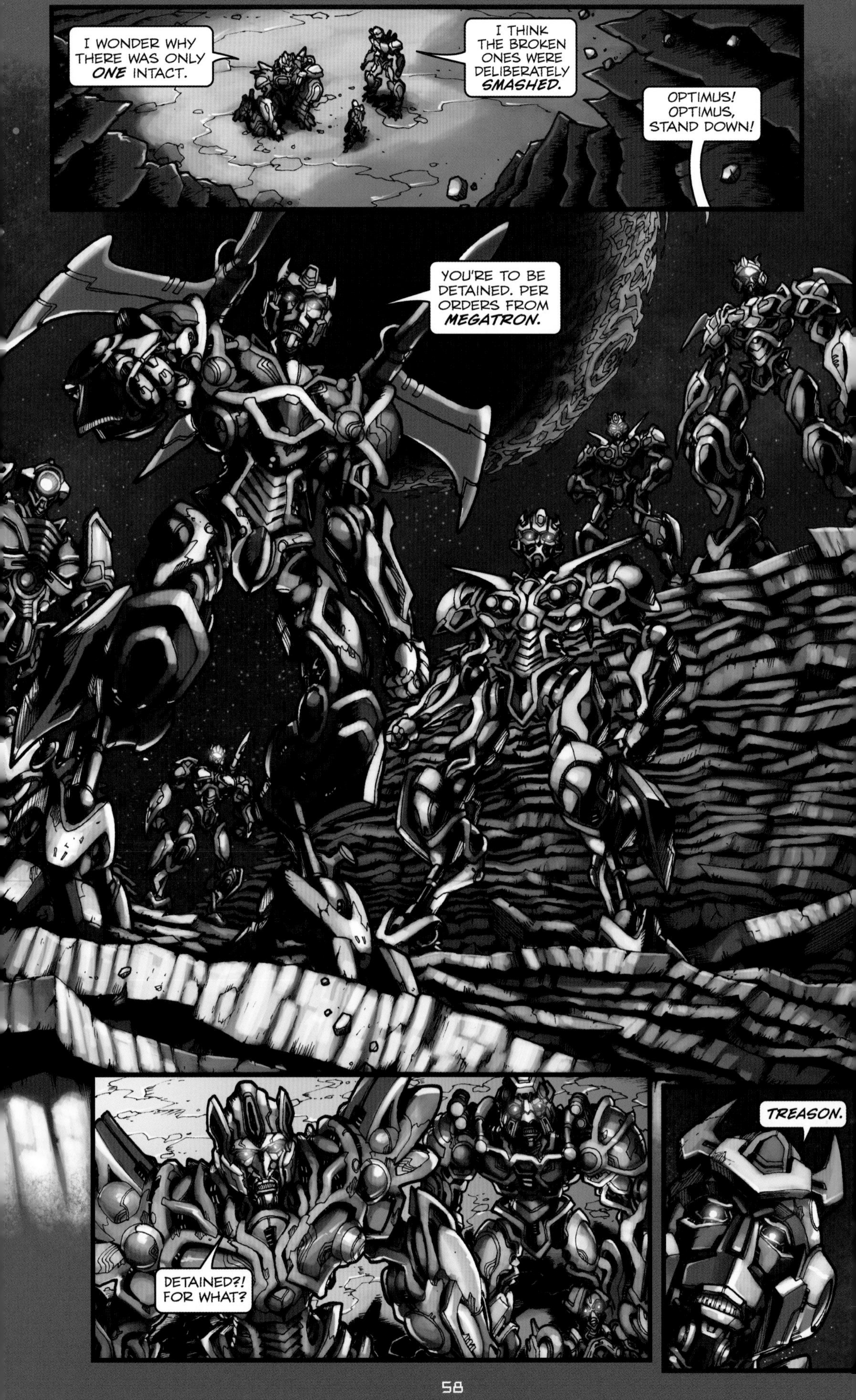

I WONDER WHY THERE WAS ONLY ONE INTACT.
I THINK THE BROKEN ONES WERE DELIBERATELY SMASHED.
OPTIMUS! OPTIMUS, STAND DOWN!
YOU'RE TO BE DETAINED. PER ORDERS FROM MEGATRON.
DETAINED?! FOR WHAT?
TREASON.

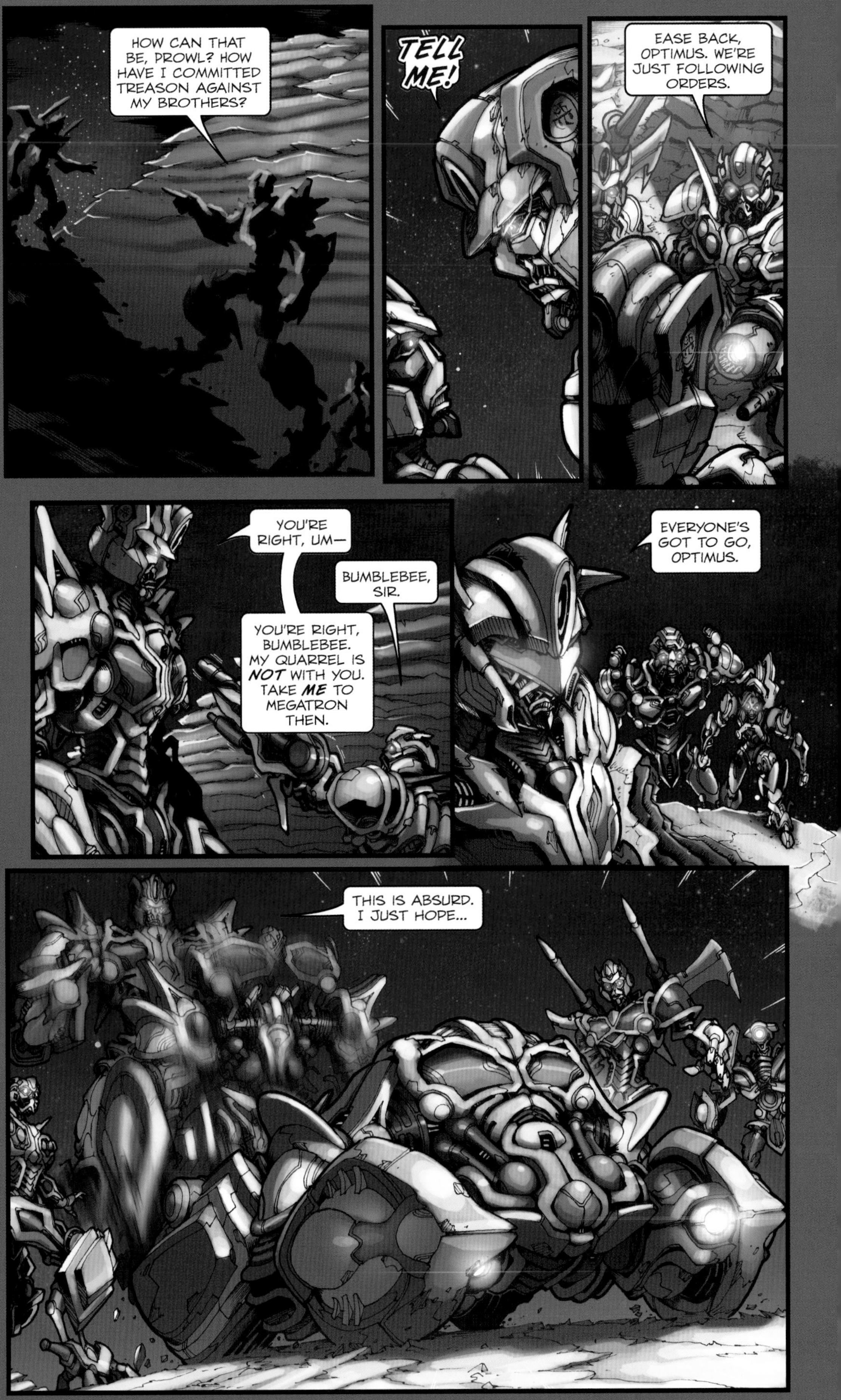

HOW CAN THAT BE, PROWL? HOW HAVE I COMMITTED TREASON AGAINST MY BROTHERS?
TELL ME!
EASE BACK, OPTIMUS. WE'RE JUST FOLLOWING ORDERS.
YOU'RE RIGHT, UM—
BUMBLEBEE, SIR.
YOU'RE RIGHT, BUMBLEBEE. MY QUARREL IS NOT WITH YOU. TAKE ME TO MEGATRON THEN.
EVERYONE'S GOT TO GO, OPTIMUS.
THIS IS ABSURD. I JUST HOPE...

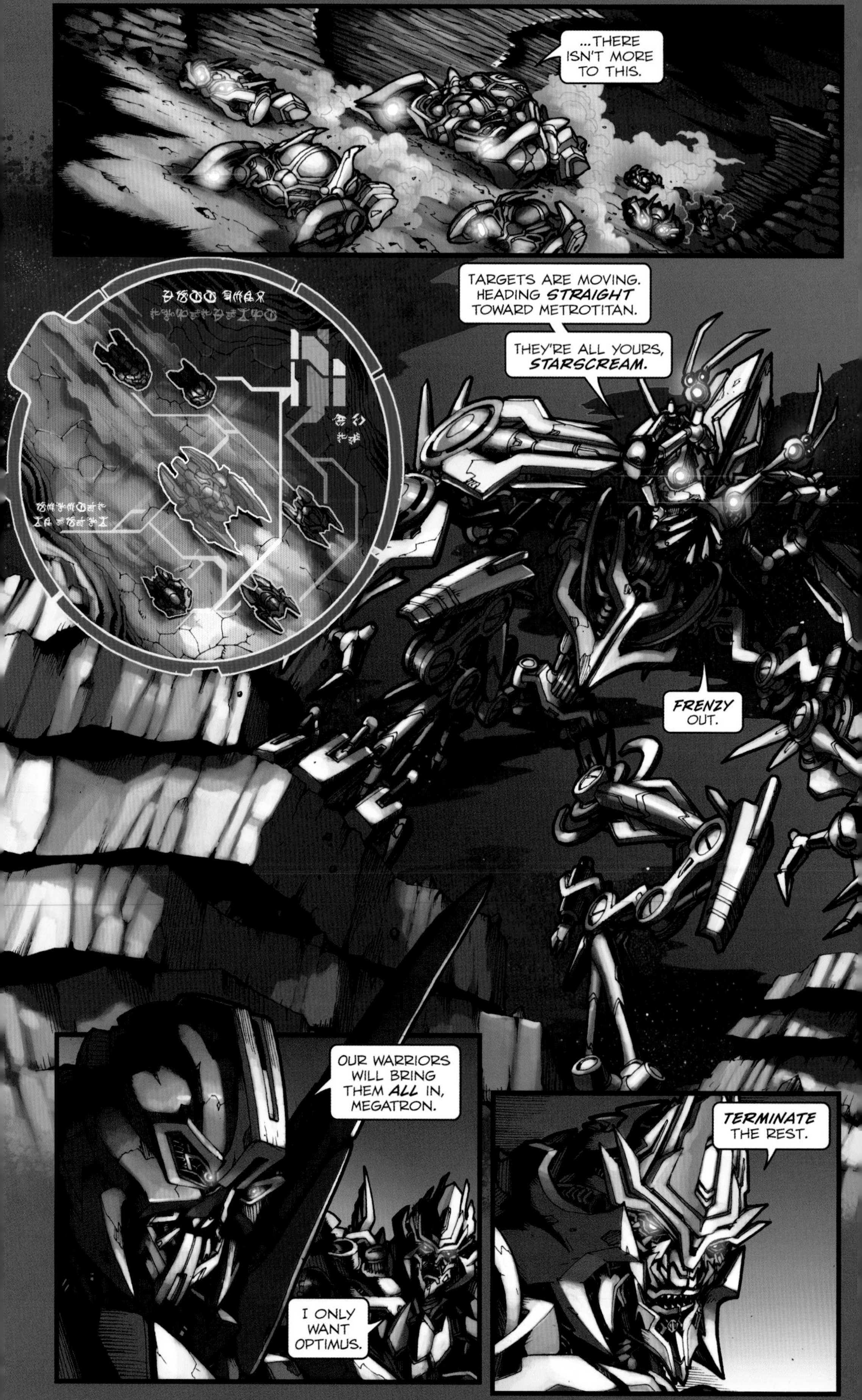
...THERE ISN'T MORE TO THIS.
TARGETS ARE MOVING. HEADING STRAIGHT TOWARD METROTITAN.
THEY'RE ALL YOURS, STARSCREAM.
FRENZY OUT.
OUR WARRIORS WILL BRING THEM ALL IN, MEGATRON.
I ONLY WANT OPTIMUS.
TERMINATE THE REST.

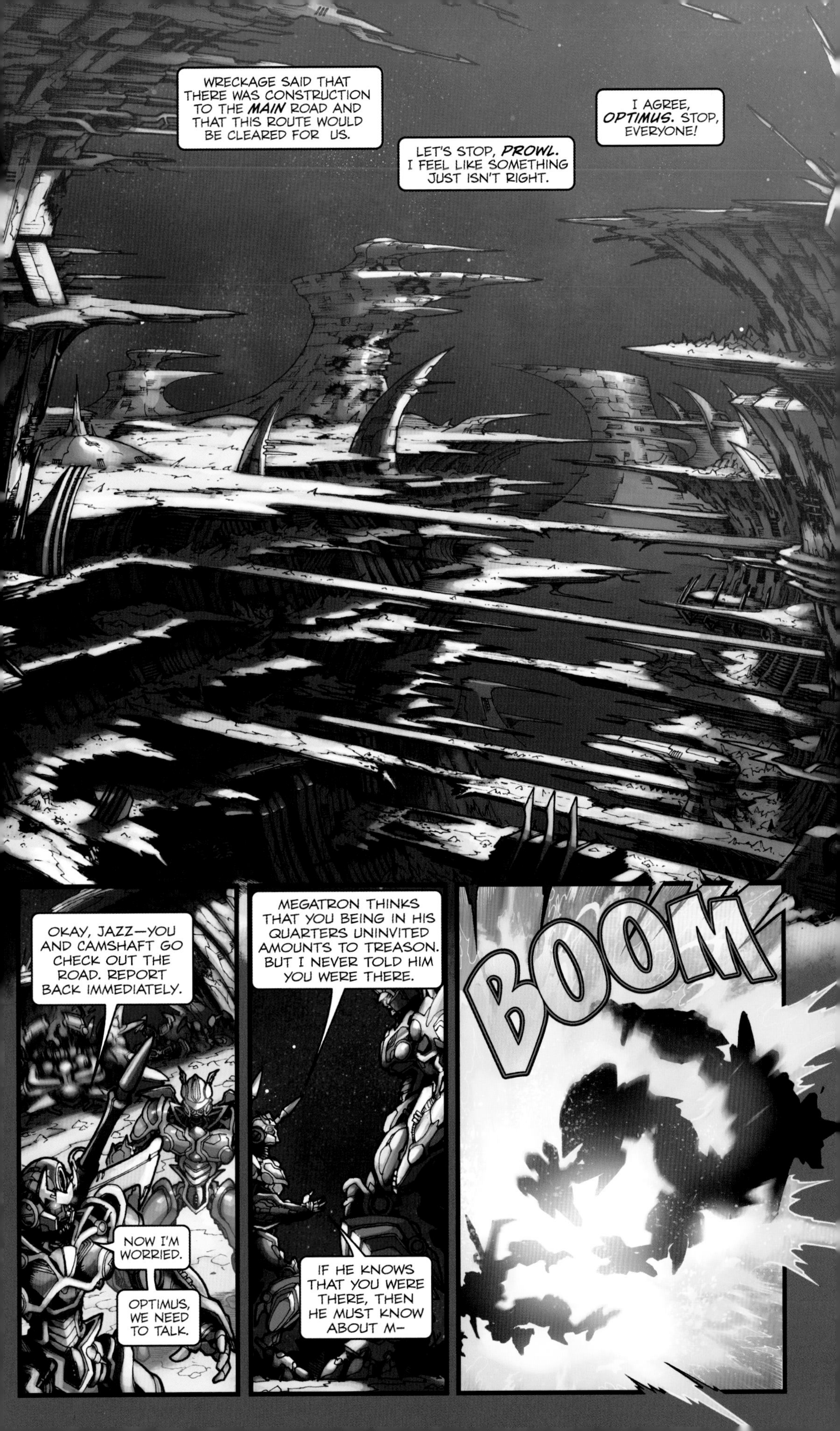
WRECKAGE SAID THAT THERE WAS CONSTRUCTION TO THE MAIN ROAD AND THAT THIS ROUTE WOULD BE CLEARED FOR US.
LET'S STOP, PROWL. I FEEL LIKE SOMETHING JUST ISN'T RIGHT.
I AGREE, OPTIMUS. STOP, EVERYONE!
OKAY, JAZZ—YOU AND CAMSHAFT GO CHECK OUT THE ROAD. REPORT BACK IMMEDIATELY.
NOW I'M WORRIED.
OPTIMUS, WE NEED TO TALK.
MEGATRON THINKS THAT YOU BEING IN HIS QUARTERS UNINVITED AMOUNTS TO TREASON. BUT I NEVER TOLD HIM YOU WERE THERE.
IF HE KNOWS THAT YOU WERE THERE, THEN HE MUST KNOW ABOUT M—
BOOM

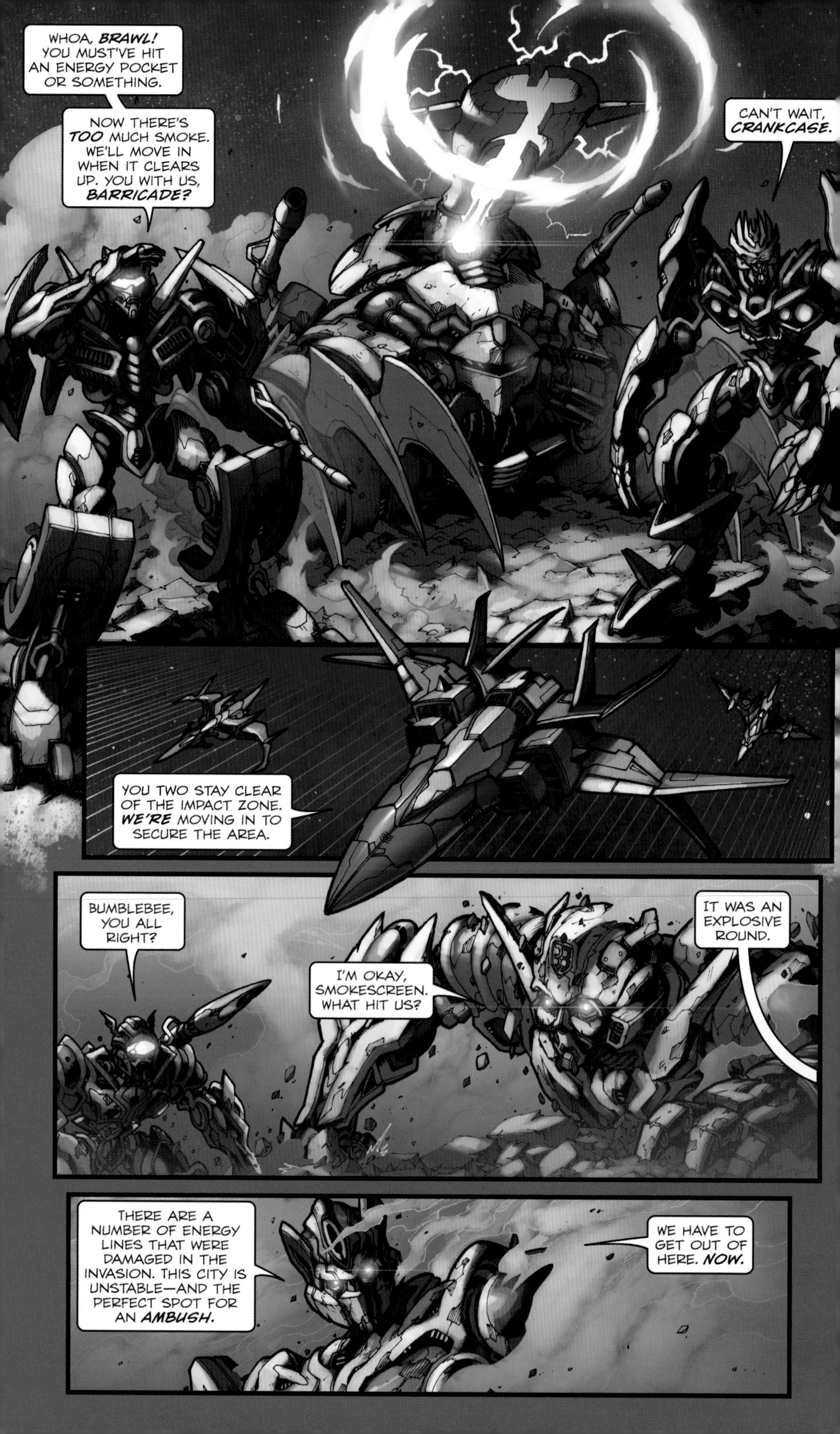
WHOA, BRAWL! YOU MUST'VE HIT AN ENERGY POCKET OR SOMETHING.
NOW THERE'S TOO MUCH SMOKE. WE'LL MOVE IN WHEN IT CLEARS UP. YOU WITH US, BARRICADE?
CAN'T WAIT, CRANKCASE.
YOU TWO STAY CLEAR OF THE IMPACT ZONE. WE'RE MOVING IN TO SECURE THE AREA.
BUMBLEBEE, YOU ALL RIGHT?
I'M OKAY, SMOKESCREEN. WHAT HIT US?
IT WAS AN EXPLOSIVE ROUND.
THERE ARE A NUMBER OF ENERGY LINES THAT WERE DAMAGED IN THE INVASION. THIS CITY IS UNSTABLE—AND THE PERFECT SPOT FOR AN AMBUSH.
WE HAVE TO GET OUT OF HERE. NOW.

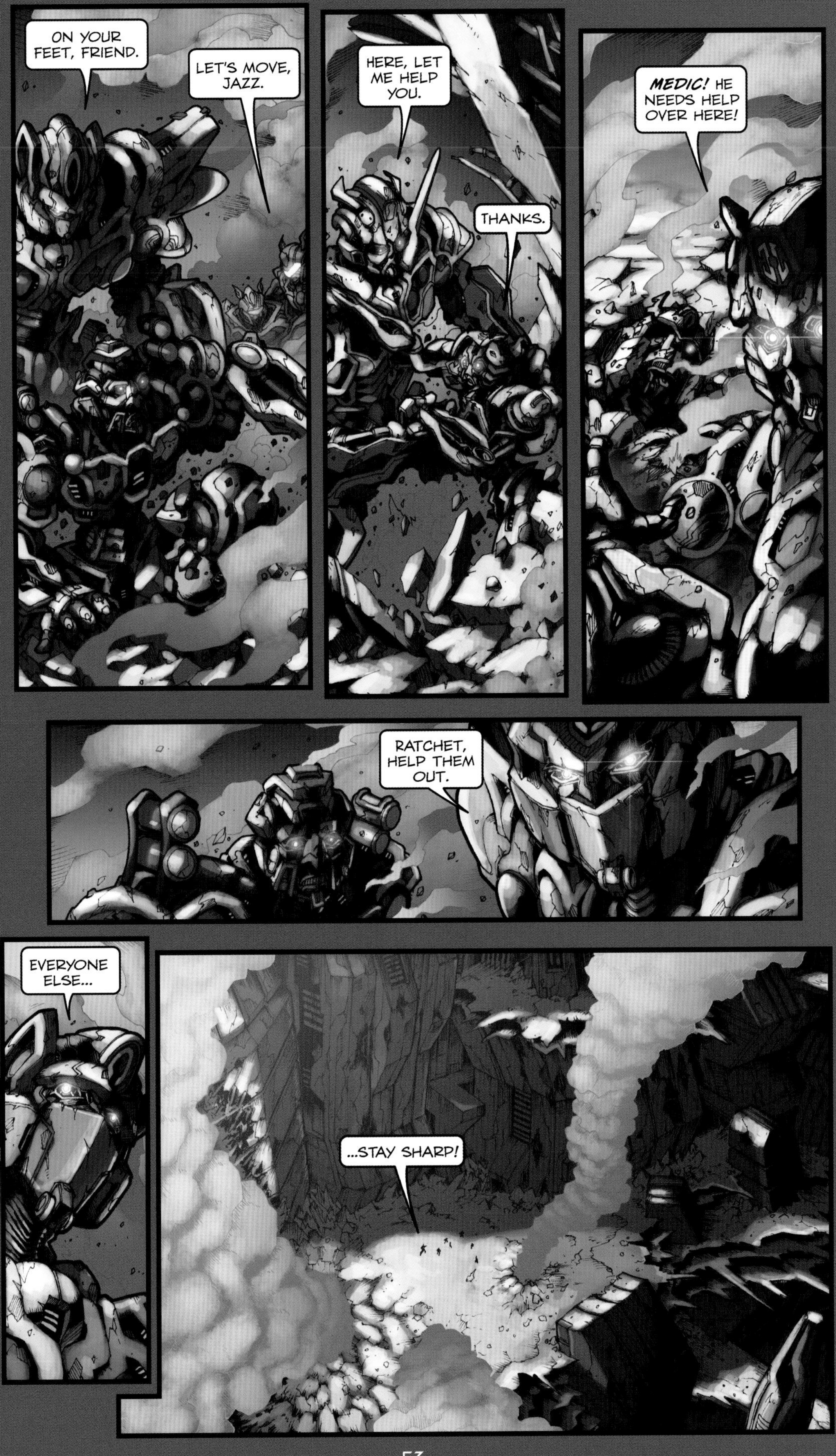
ON YOUR FEET, FRIEND.
LET'S MOVE, JAZZ.
HERE, LET ME HELP YOU.
THANKS.
MEDIC! HE NEEDS HELP OVER HERE!
RATCHET, HELP THEM OUT.
EVERYONE ELSE...
...STAY SHARP!

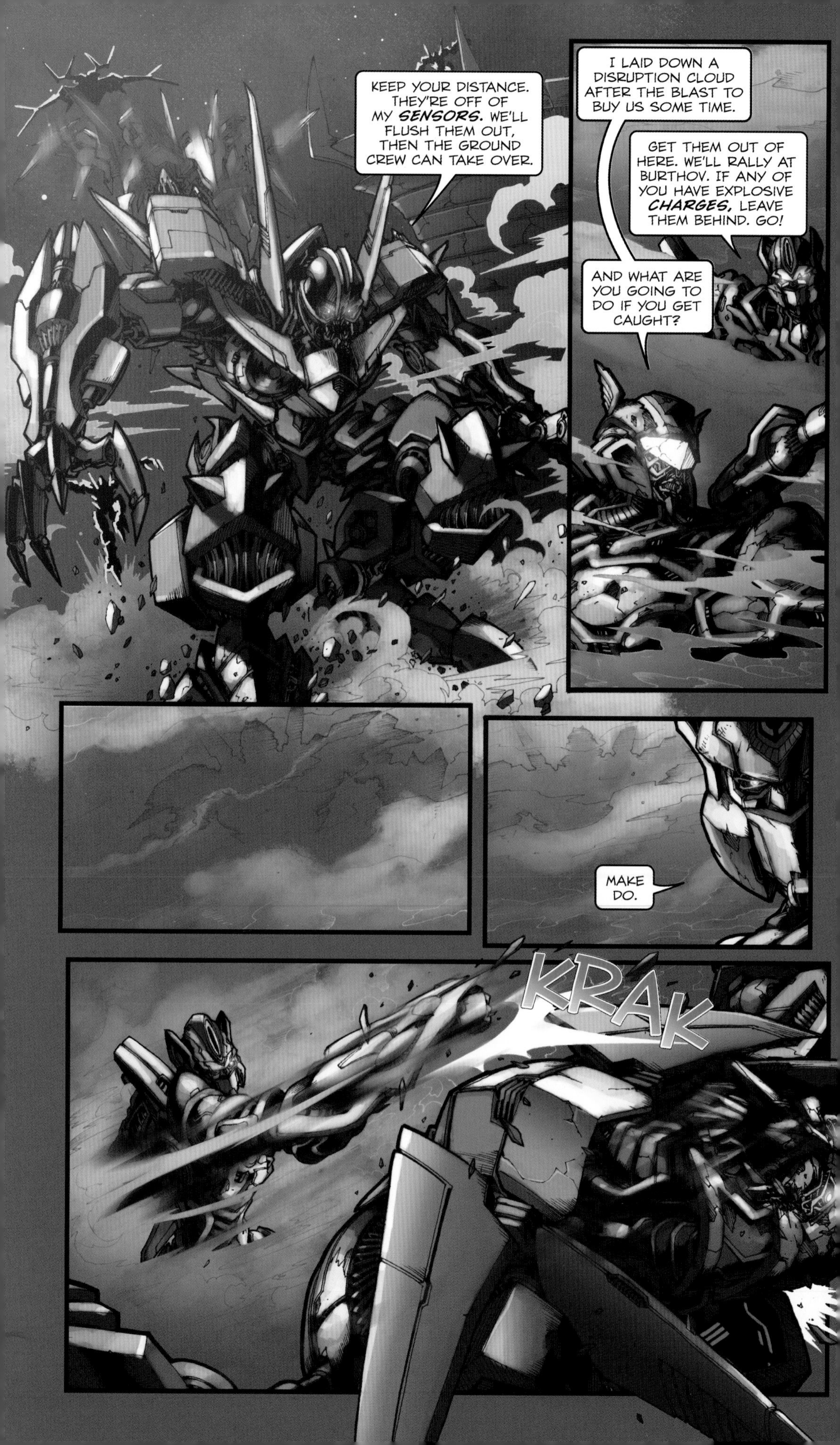
KEEP YOUR DISTANCE. THEY'RE OFF OF MY **SENSORS.** WE'LL FLUSH THEM OUT, THEN THE GROUND CREW CAN TAKE OVER.
I LAID DOWN A DISRUPTION CLOUD AFTER THE BLAST TO BUY US SOME TIME.
GET THEM OUT OF HERE. WE'LL RALLY AT BURTHOV. IF ANY OF YOU HAVE EXPLOSIVE **CHARGES,** LEAVE THEM BEHIND. GO!
AND WHAT ARE YOU GOING TO DO IF YOU GET CAUGHT?
MAKE DO.
KRAK

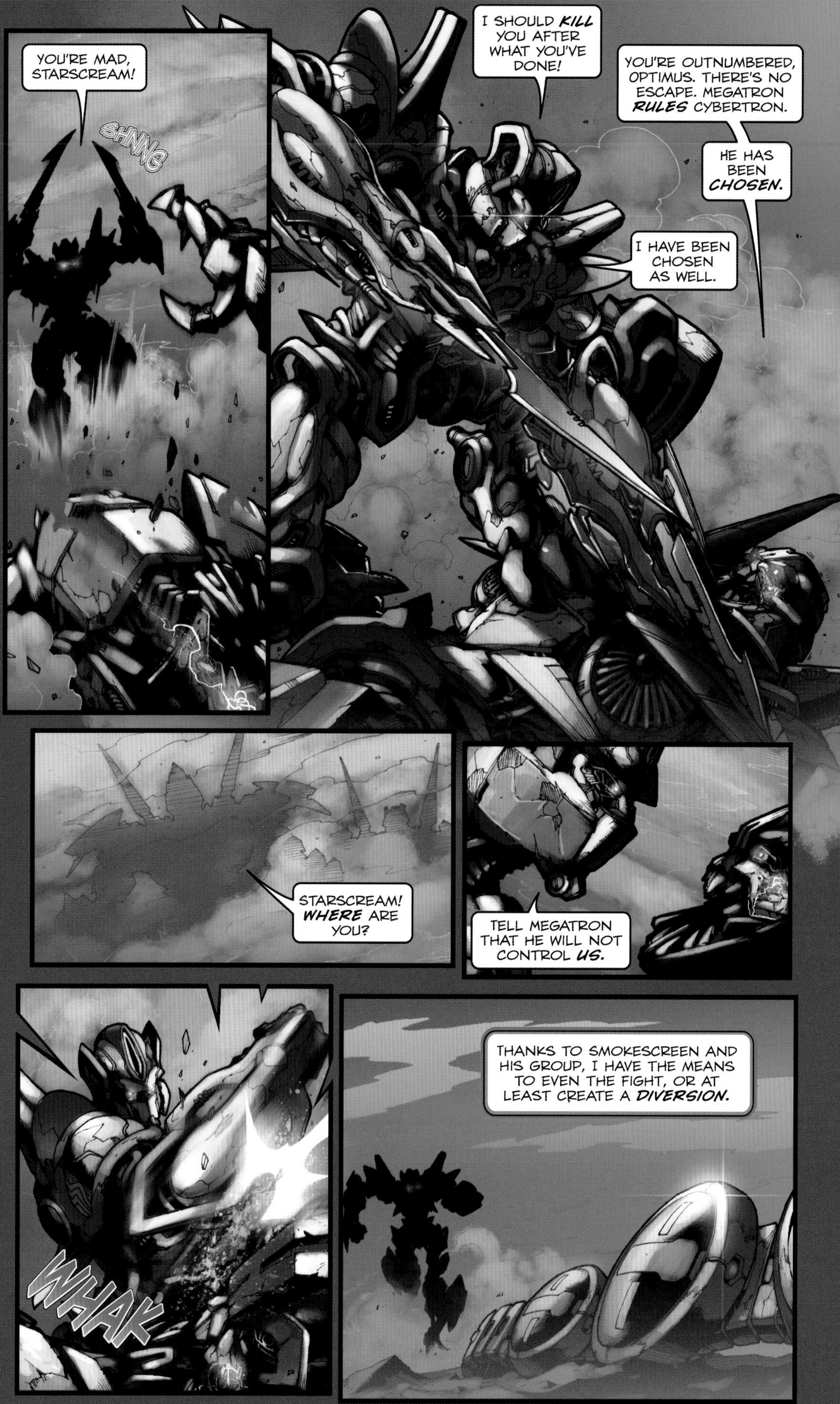
YOU'RE MAD, STARSCREAM!
SHNNG
I SHOULD KILL YOU AFTER WHAT YOU'VE DONE!
YOU'RE OUTNUMBERED, OPTIMUS. THERE'S NO ESCAPE. MEGATRON RULES CYBERTRON.
HE HAS BEEN CHOSEN.
I HAVE BEEN CHOSEN AS WELL.
STARSCREAM! WHERE ARE YOU?
TELL MEGATRON THAT HE WILL NOT CONTROL US.
WHAK
THANKS TO SMOKESCREEN AND HIS GROUP, I HAVE THE MEANS TO EVEN THE FIGHT, OR AT LEAST CREATE A DIVERSION.

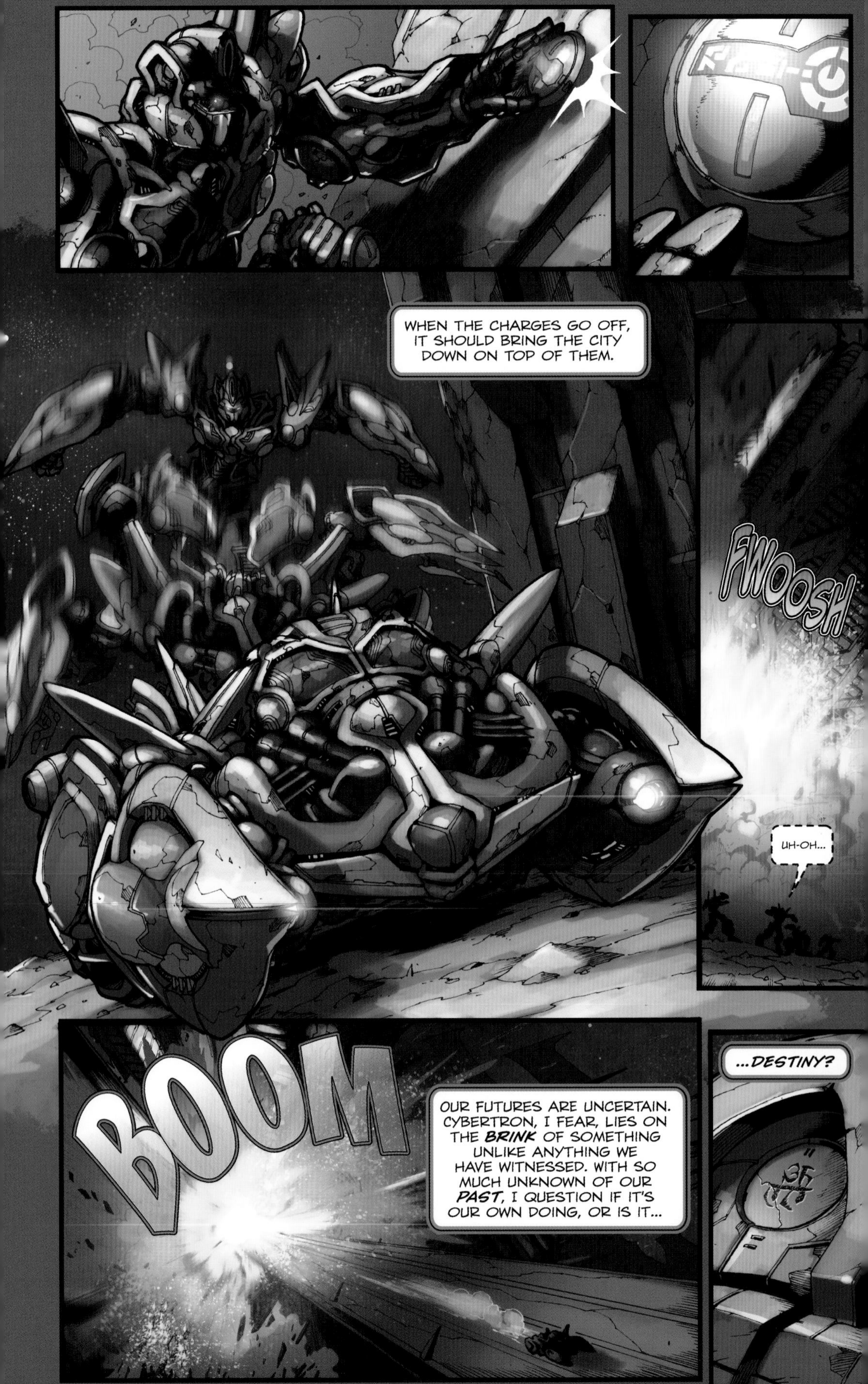

WHEN THE CHARGES GO OFF, IT SHOULD BRING THE CITY DOWN ON TOP OF THEM.
FWOOSH
UH-OH...
BOOM
OUR FUTURES ARE UNCERTAIN. CYBERTRON, I FEAR, LIES ON THE *BRINK* OF SOMETHING UNLIKE ANYTHING WE HAVE WITNESSED. WITH SO MUCH UNKNOWN OF OUR *PAST*, I QUESTION IF IT'S OUR OWN DOING, OR IS IT...
...DESTINY?

LATER IN TRYPTICON.

MY WARRIORS OF CYBERTRON. WE HAVE REMAINED *PEACEFUL* FOR TOO LONG. WHERE HAS THE PATH OF CIVILITY BROUGHT US?

ATTACKS FROM BEYOND OUR PLANET—AND FROM OUR OWN KIND. BETRAYED BY OUR OWN BROTHERS!

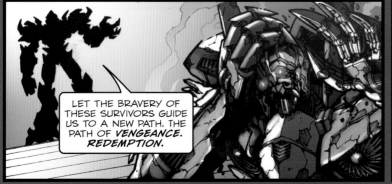

LET THE BRAVERY OF THESE SURVIVORS GUIDE US TO A NEW PATH. THE PATH OF *VENGEANCE. REDEMPTION.*

DEFIANCE!

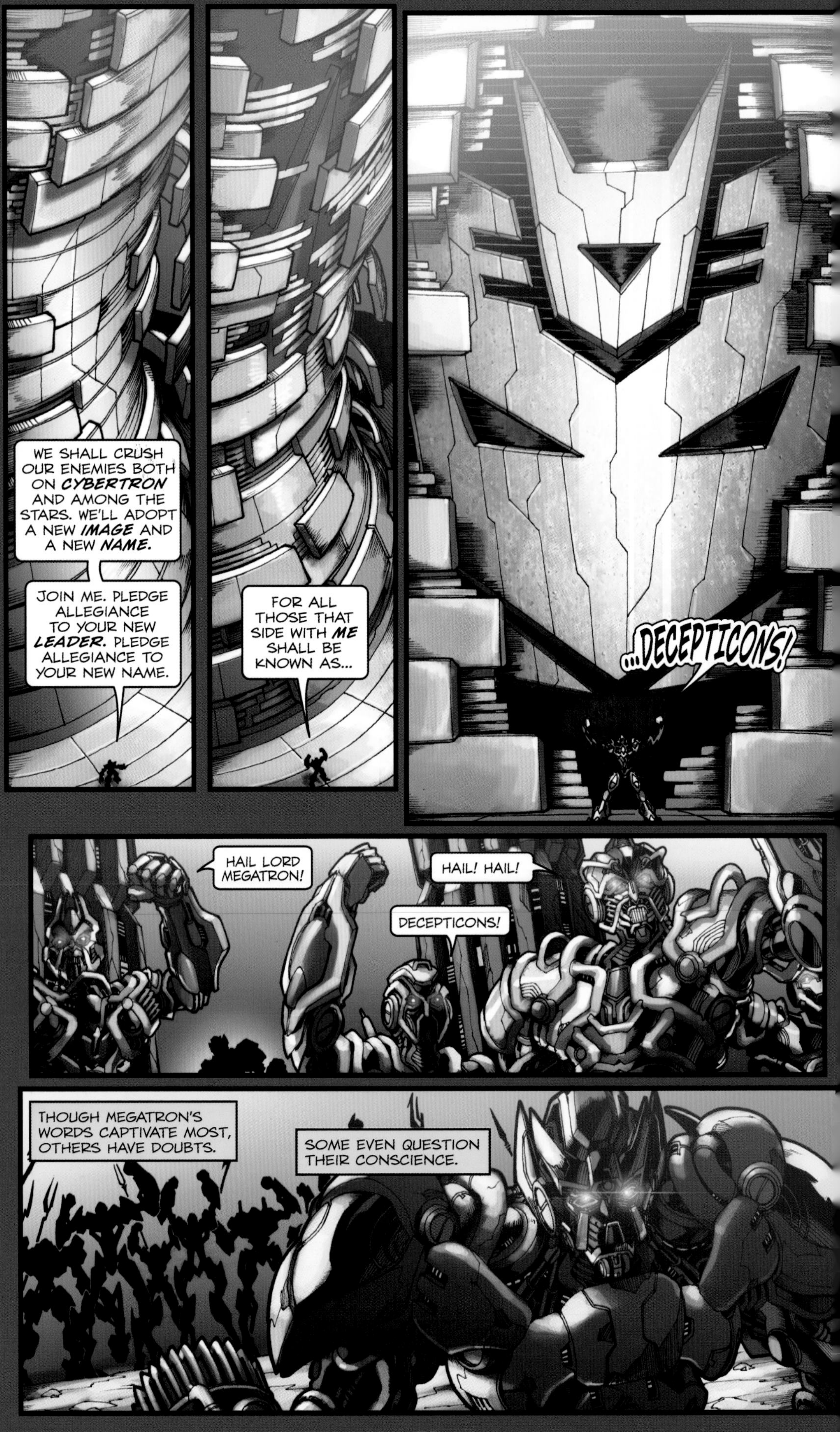

WE SHALL CRUSH OUR ENEMIES BOTH ON CYBERTRON AND AMONG THE STARS. WE'LL ADOPT A NEW IMAGE AND A NEW NAME.
JOIN ME. PLEDGE ALLEGIANCE TO YOUR NEW LEADER. PLEDGE ALLEGIANCE TO YOUR NEW NAME.
FOR ALL THOSE THAT SIDE WITH ME SHALL BE KNOWN AS...
...DECEPTICONS!
HAIL LORD MEGATRON!
HAIL! HAIL!
DECEPTICONS!
THOUGH MEGATRON'S WORDS CAPTIVATE MOST, OTHERS HAVE DOUBTS.
SOME EVEN QUESTION THEIR CONSCIENCE.

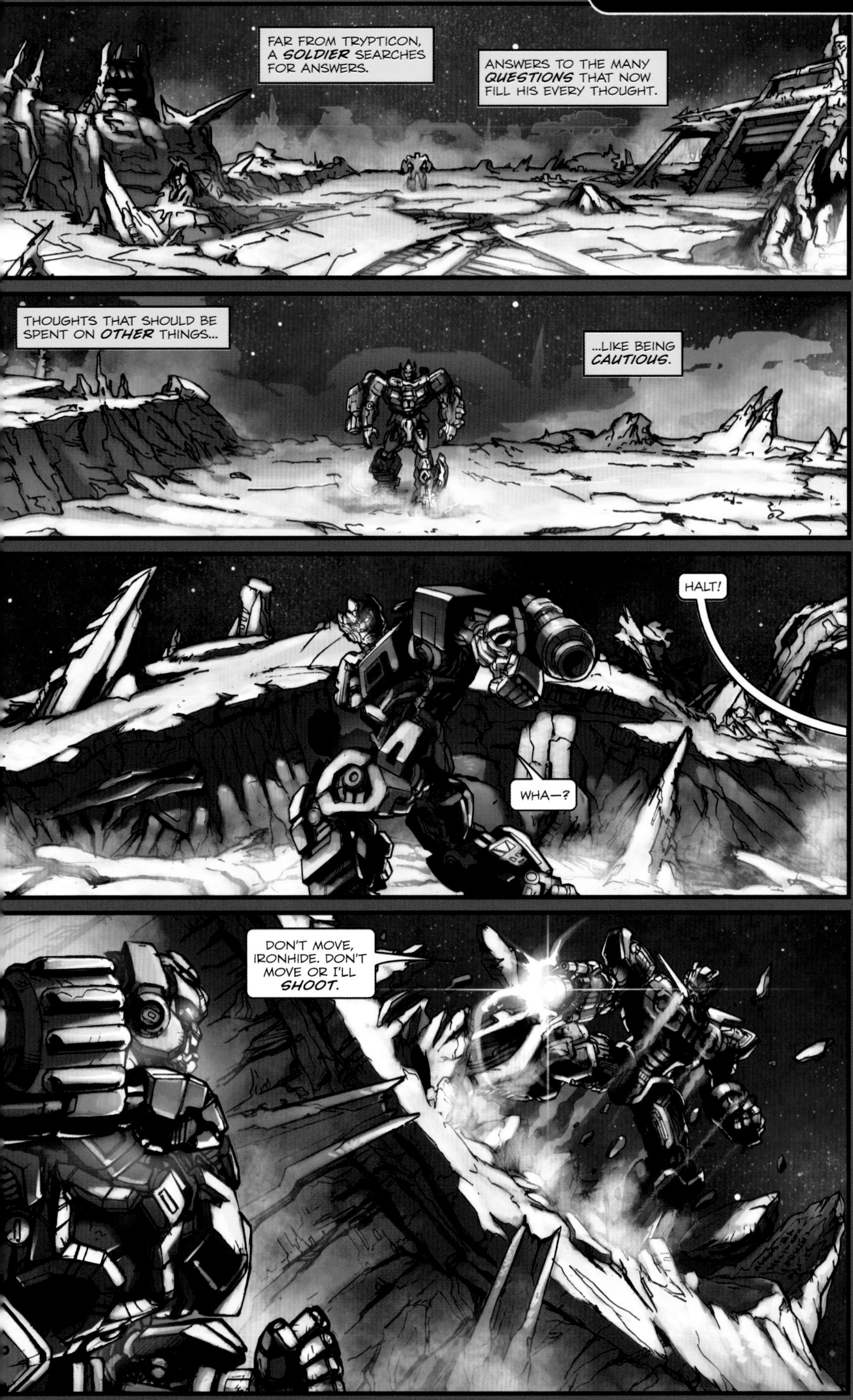
FAR FROM TRYPTICON, A SOLDIER SEARCHES FOR ANSWERS.
ANSWERS TO THE MANY QUESTIONS THAT NOW FILL HIS EVERY THOUGHT.
THOUGHTS THAT SHOULD BE SPENT ON OTHER THINGS...
...LIKE BEING CAUTIOUS.
HALT!
WHA—?
DON'T MOVE, IRONHIDE. DON'T MOVE OR I'LL SHOOT.

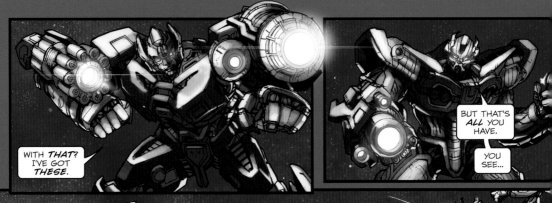

WITH *THAT?* I'VE GOT *THESE.*

BUT THAT'S *ALL* YOU HAVE.

YOU SEE...

...I'VE GOT *THEM.*

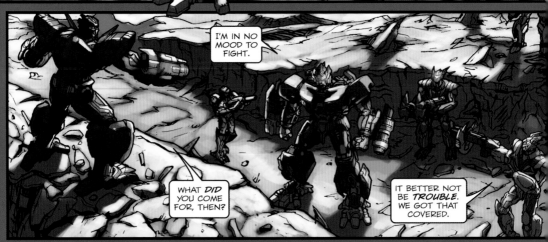

I'M IN NO MOOD TO FIGHT.

WHAT *DID* YOU COME FOR, THEN?

IT BETTER NOT BE *TROUBLE.* WE GOT THAT COVERED.

I'M JUST WALKING. THERE'S NOTHING BACK THERE FOR ME NOW.

THE CAUSE HAS CHANGED.

IT'S IRONHIDE. HE'S *ALONE.*

VERY WELL, BRING HIM DOWN. *PRIME* WANTS TO SEE HIM.

RIGHT AWAY.

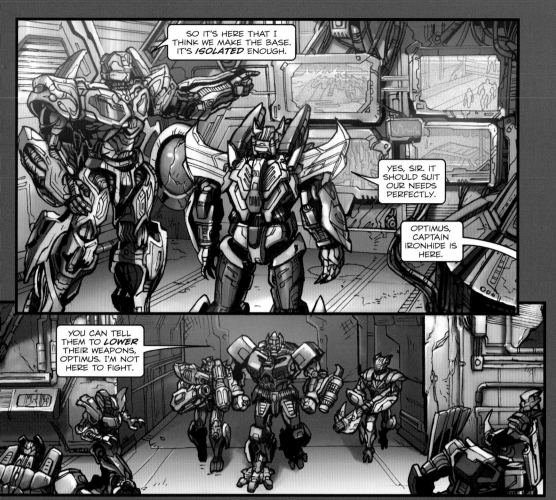

SO IT'S HERE THAT I THINK WE MAKE THE BASE. IT'S *ISOLATED* ENOUGH.

YES, SIR. IT SHOULD SUIT OUR NEEDS PERFECTLY.

OPTIMUS, CAPTAIN IRONHIDE IS HERE.

YOU CAN TELL THEM TO *LOWER* THEIR WEAPONS, OPTIMUS. I'M NOT HERE TO FIGHT.

THEN WHAT *ARE* YOU HERE FOR, IRONHIDE?

I'M HERE TO *JOIN* YOU.

YOU'LL *NEED* MY HELP, TOO.

MEGATRON IS FORMING AN ARMY, AND HE'S FINDING NO TROUBLE IN FILLING THE RANKS.

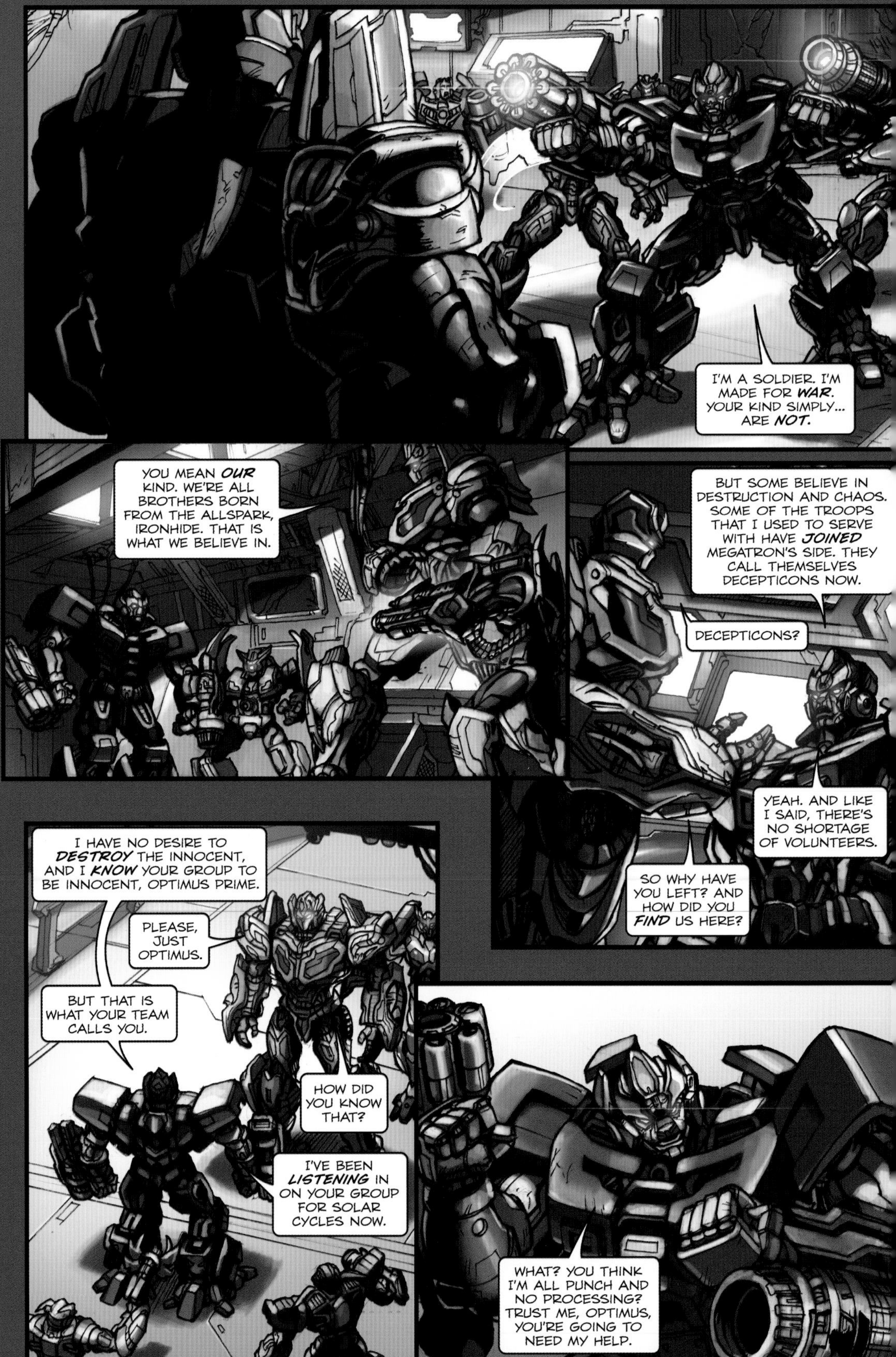
I'M A SOLDIER. I'M MADE FOR WAR. YOUR KIND SIMPLY... ARE NOT.
YOU MEAN OUR KIND. WE'RE ALL BROTHERS BORN FROM THE ALLSPARK, IRONHIDE. THAT IS WHAT WE BELIEVE IN.
BUT SOME BELIEVE IN DESTRUCTION AND CHAOS. SOME OF THE TROOPS THAT I USED TO SERVE WITH HAVE JOINED MEGATRON'S SIDE. THEY CALL THEMSELVES DECEPTICONS NOW.
DECEPTICONS?
YEAH. AND LIKE I SAID, THERE'S NO SHORTAGE OF VOLUNTEERS.
SO WHY HAVE YOU LEFT? AND HOW DID YOU FIND US HERE?
I HAVE NO DESIRE TO DESTROY THE INNOCENT, AND I KNOW YOUR GROUP TO BE INNOCENT, OPTIMUS PRIME.
PLEASE, JUST OPTIMUS.
BUT THAT IS WHAT YOUR TEAM CALLS YOU.
HOW DID YOU KNOW THAT?
I'VE BEEN LISTENING IN ON YOUR GROUP FOR SOLAR CYCLES NOW.
WHAT? YOU THINK I'M ALL PUNCH AND NO PROCESSING? TRUST ME, OPTIMUS, YOU'RE GOING TO NEED MY HELP.

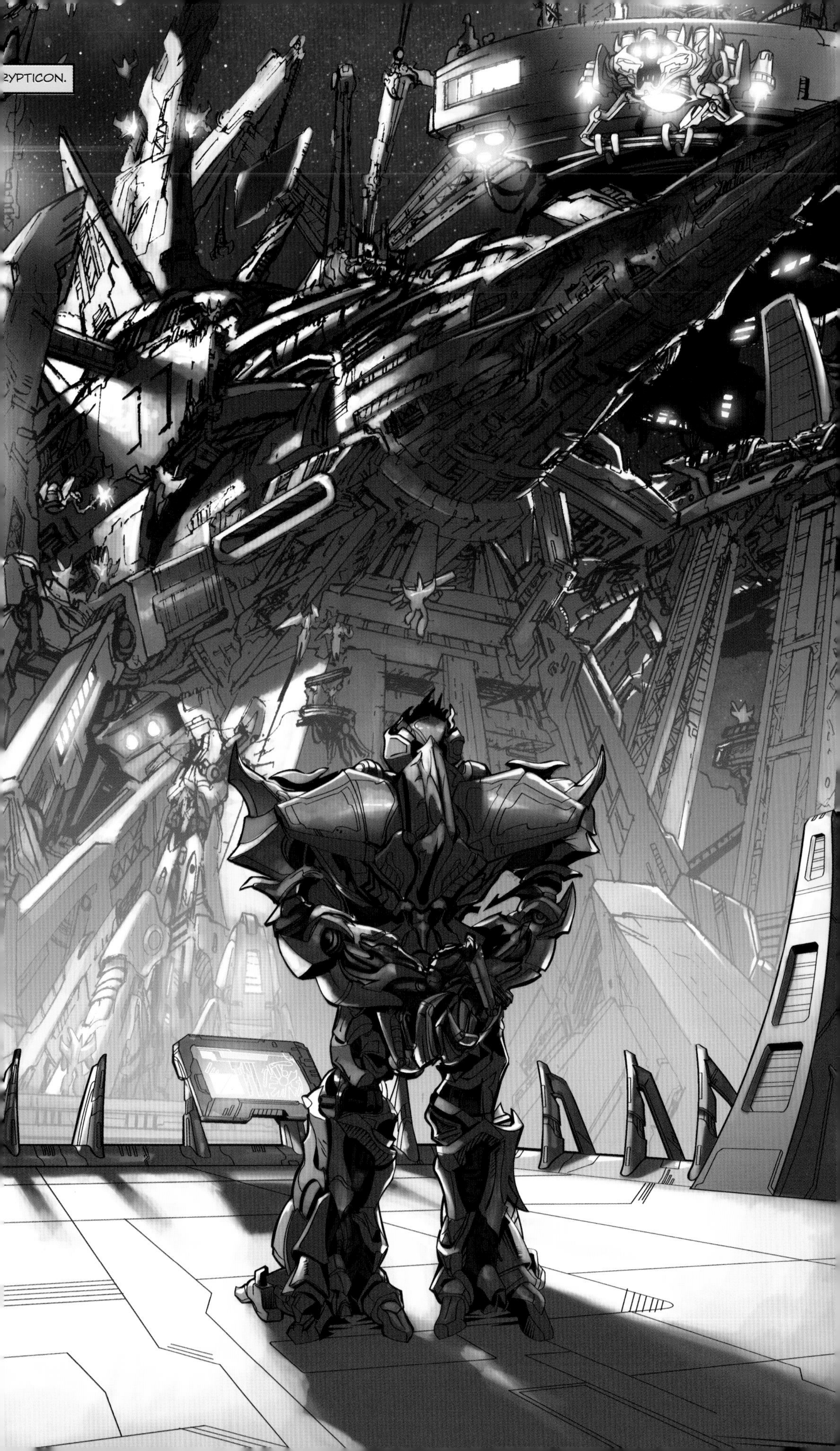

RYPTICON.

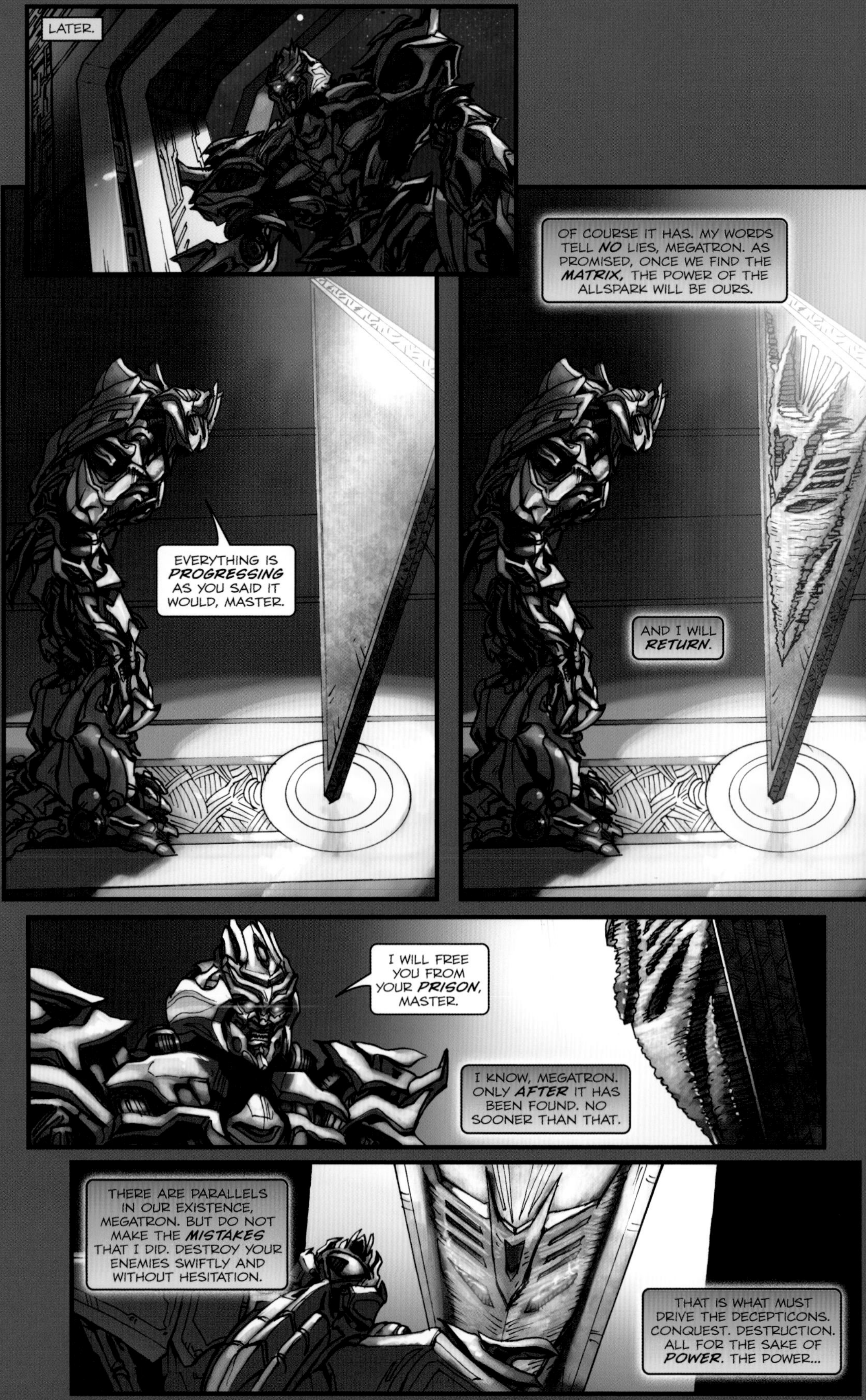
LATER.
EVERYTHING IS PROGRESSING AS YOU SAID IT WOULD, MASTER.
OF COURSE IT HAS. MY WORDS TELL NO LIES, MEGATRON. AS PROMISED, ONCE WE FIND THE MATRIX, THE POWER OF THE ALLSPARK WILL BE OURS.
AND I WILL RETURN.
I WILL FREE YOU FROM YOUR PRISON, MASTER.
I KNOW, MEGATRON. ONLY AFTER IT HAS BEEN FOUND. NO SOONER THAN THAT.
THERE ARE PARALLELS IN OUR EXISTENCE, MEGATRON. BUT DO NOT MAKE THE MISTAKES THAT I DID. DESTROY YOUR ENEMIES SWIFTLY AND WITHOUT HESITATION.
THAT IS WHAT MUST DRIVE THE DECEPTICONS. CONQUEST. DESTRUCTION. ALL FOR THE SAKE OF POWER. THE POWER...

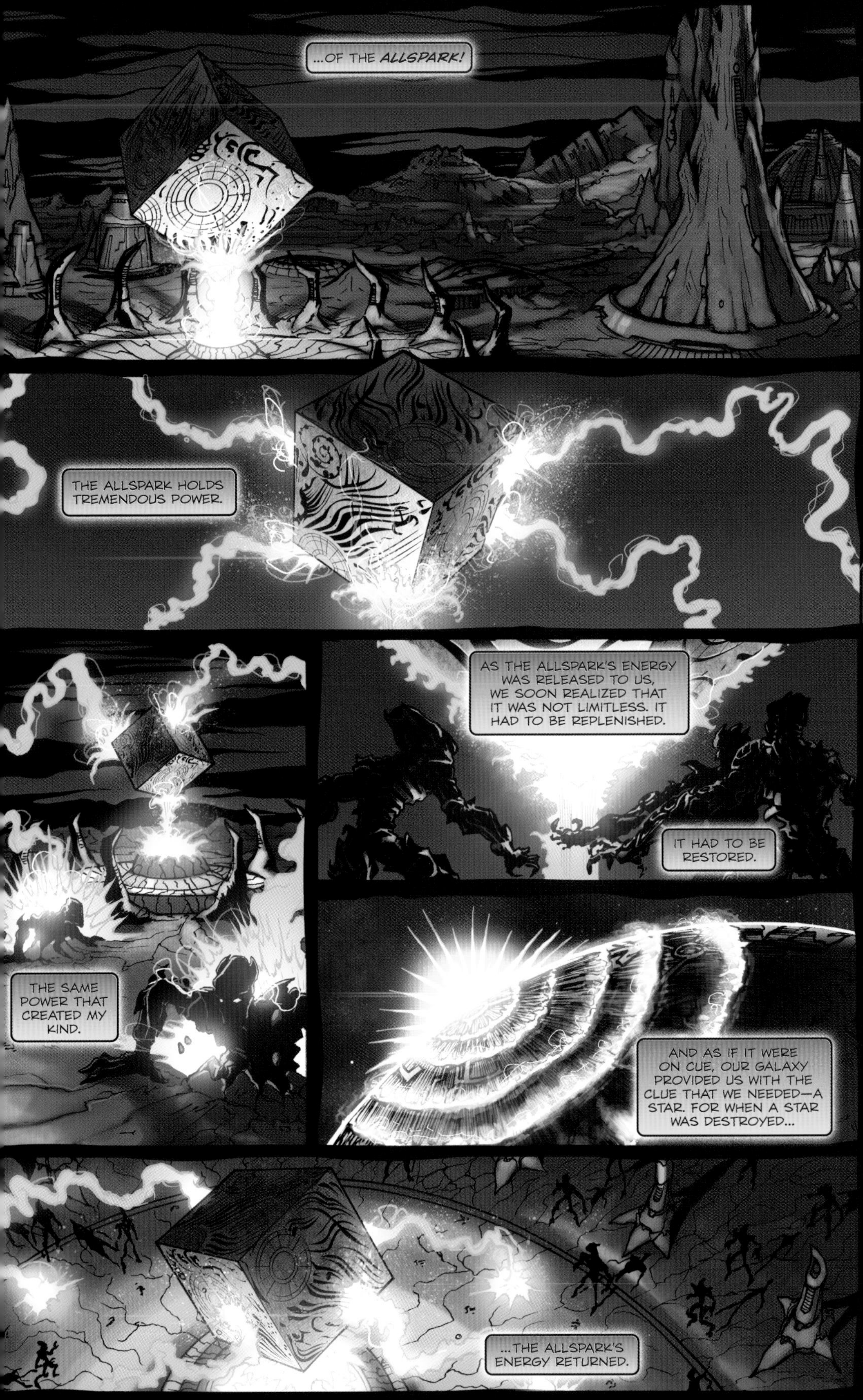
...OF THE *ALLSPARK!*
THE ALLSPARK HOLDS TREMENDOUS POWER.
THE SAME POWER THAT CREATED MY KIND.
AS THE ALLSPARK'S ENERGY WAS RELEASED TO US, WE SOON REALIZED THAT IT WAS NOT LIMITLESS. IT HAD TO BE REPLENISHED.
IT HAD TO BE RESTORED.
AND AS IF IT WERE ON CUE, OUR GALAXY PROVIDED US WITH THE CLUE THAT WE NEEDED—A STAR. FOR WHEN A STAR WAS DESTROYED...
...THE ALLSPARK'S ENERGY RETURNED.

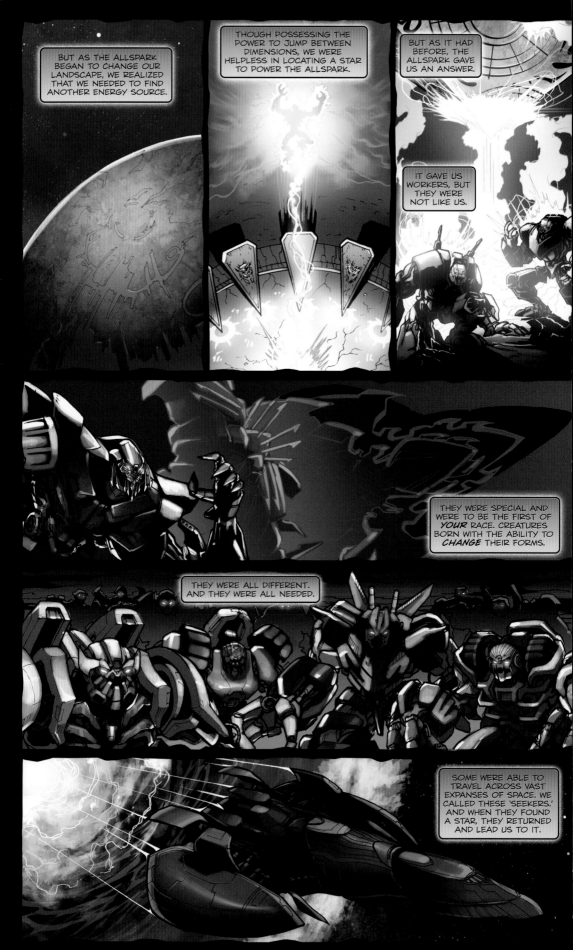

BUT AS THE ALLSPARK BEGAN TO CHANGE OUR LANDSCAPE, WE REALIZED THAT WE NEEDED TO FIND ANOTHER ENERGY SOURCE.

THOUGH POSSESSING THE POWER TO JUMP BETWEEN DIMENSIONS, WE WERE HELPLESS IN LOCATING A STAR TO POWER THE ALLSPARK.

BUT AS IT HAD BEFORE, THE ALLSPARK GAVE US AN ANSWER.

IT GAVE US WORKERS, BUT THEY WERE NOT LIKE US.

THEY WERE SPECIAL AND WERE TO BE THE FIRST OF *YOUR* RACE. CREATURES BORN WITH THE ABILITY TO *CHANGE* THEIR FORMS.

THEY WERE ALL DIFFERENT. AND THEY WERE ALL NEEDED.

SOME WERE ABLE TO TRAVEL ACROSS VAST EXPANSES OF SPACE. WE CALLED THESE 'SEEKERS.' AND WHEN THEY FOUND A STAR, THEY RETURNED AND LEAD US TO IT.

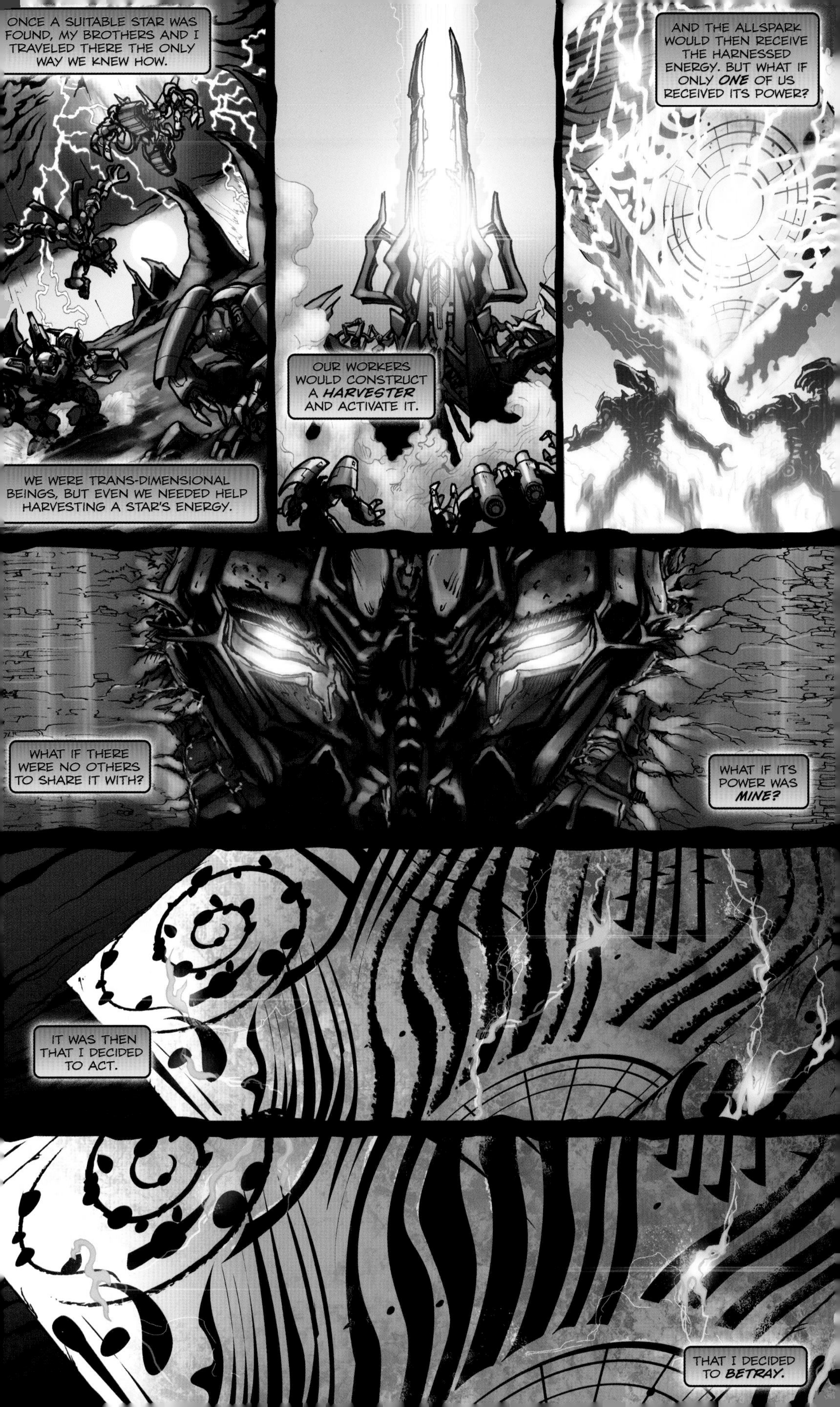
ONCE A SUITABLE STAR WAS FOUND, MY BROTHERS AND I TRAVELED THERE THE ONLY WAY WE KNEW HOW.
WE WERE TRANS-DIMENSIONAL BEINGS, BUT EVEN WE NEEDED HELP HARVESTING A STAR'S ENERGY.
OUR WORKERS WOULD CONSTRUCT A *HARVESTER* AND ACTIVATE IT.
AND THE ALLSPARK WOULD THEN RECEIVE THE HARNESSED ENERGY. BUT WHAT IF ONLY *ONE* OF US RECEIVED ITS POWER?
WHAT IF THERE WERE NO OTHERS TO SHARE IT WITH?
WHAT IF ITS POWER WAS *MINE?*
IT WAS THEN THAT I DECIDED TO ACT.
THAT I DECIDED TO *BETRAY.*

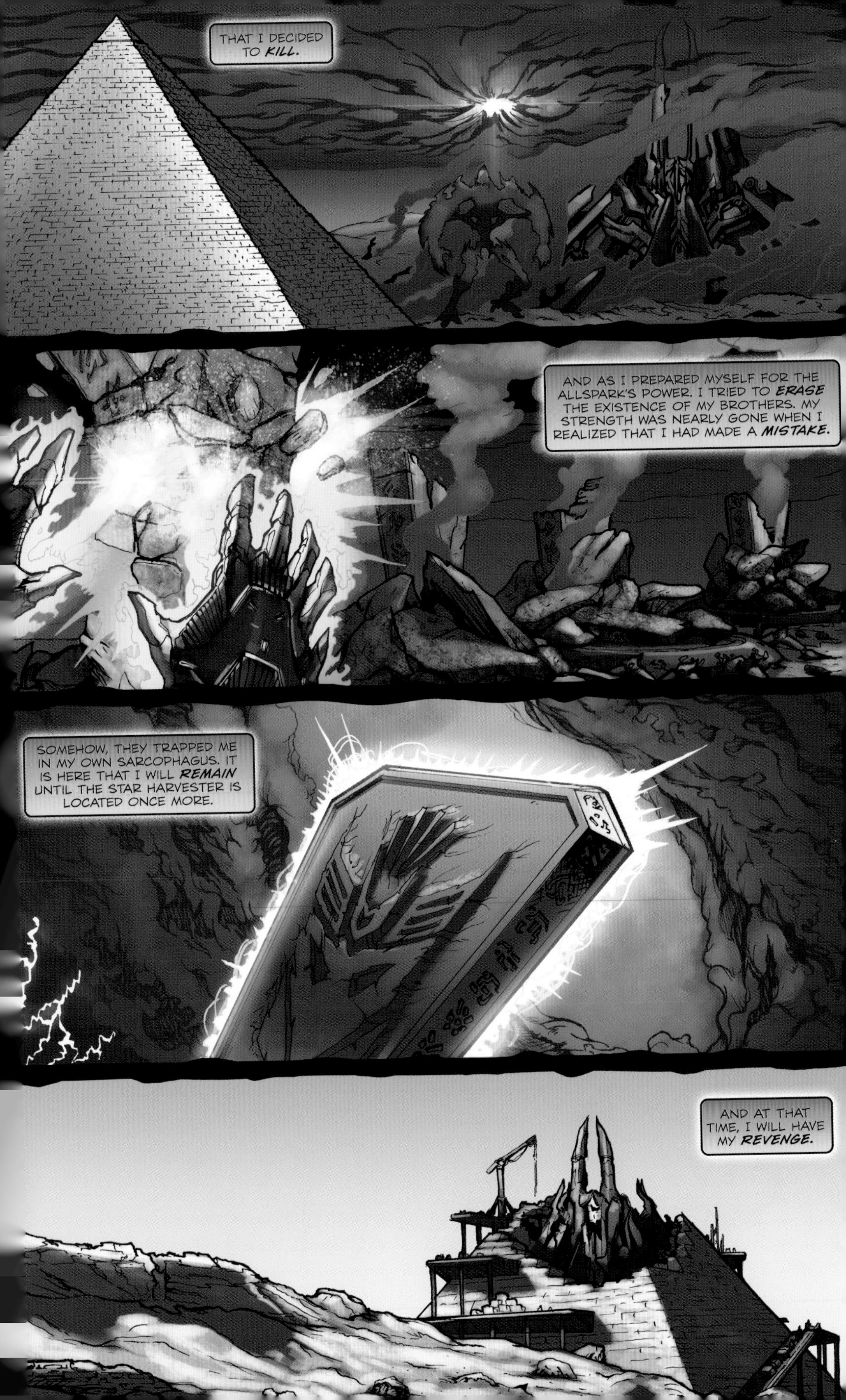
THAT I DECIDED TO KILL.
AND AS I PREPARED MYSELF FOR THE ALLSPARK'S POWER. I TRIED TO ERASE THE EXISTENCE OF MY BROTHERS. MY STRENGTH WAS NEARLY GONE WHEN I REALIZED THAT I HAD MADE A MISTAKE.
SOMEHOW, THEY TRAPPED ME IN MY OWN SARCOPHAGUS. IT IS HERE THAT I WILL REMAIN UNTIL THE STAR HARVESTER IS LOCATED ONCE MORE.
AND AT THAT TIME, I WILL HAVE MY REVENGE.

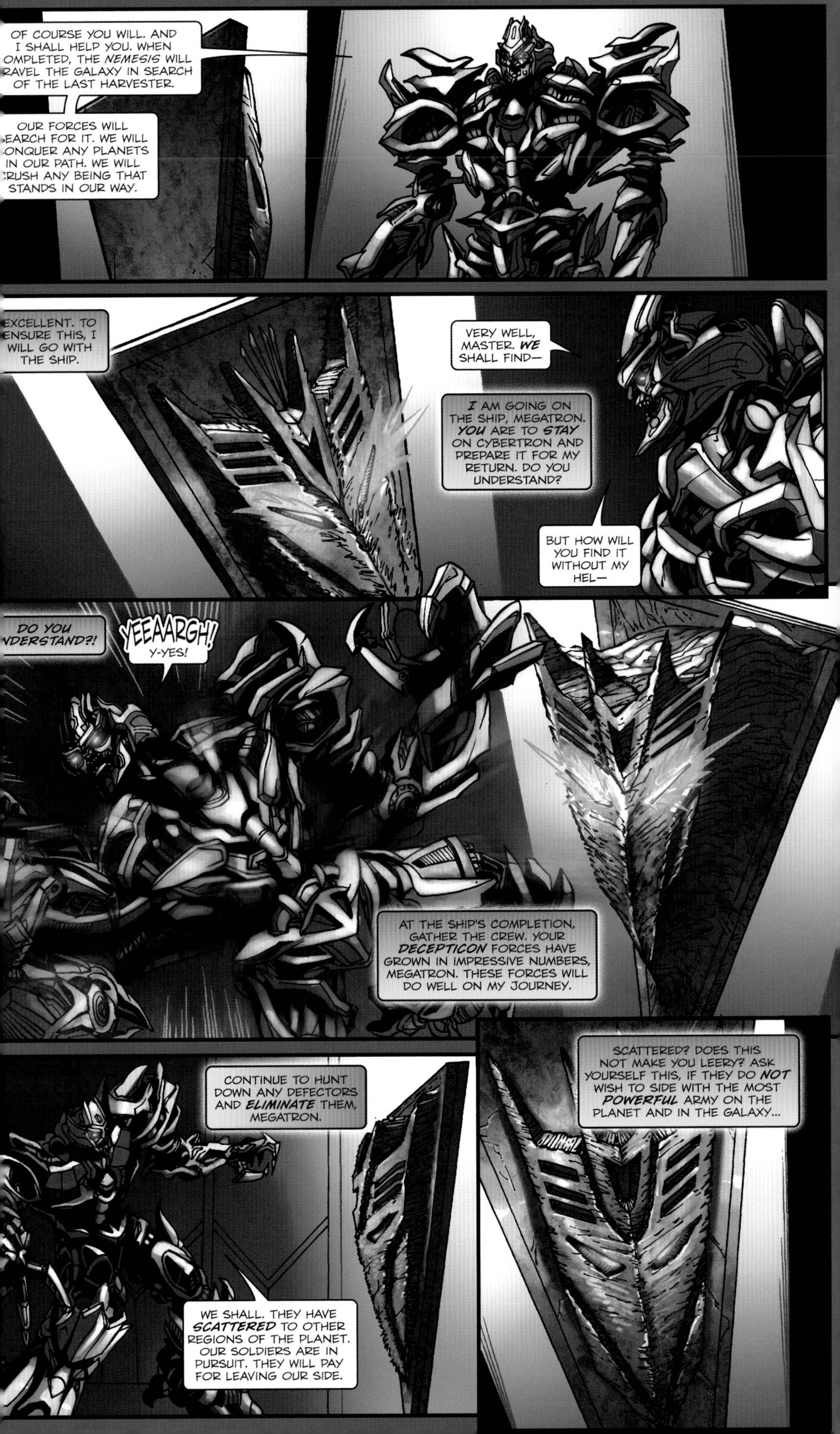

OF COURSE YOU WILL. AND I SHALL HELP YOU. WHEN OMPLETED, THE NEMESIS WILL RAVEL THE GALAXY IN SEARCH OF THE LAST HARVESTER.
OUR FORCES WILL EARCH FOR IT. WE WILL ONQUER ANY PLANETS IN OUR PATH. WE WILL RUSH ANY BEING THAT STANDS IN OUR WAY.
EXCELLENT. TO ENSURE THIS, I WILL GO WITH THE SHIP.
VERY WELL, MASTER. WE SHALL FIND—
I AM GOING ON THE SHIP, MEGATRON. YOU ARE TO STAY ON CYBERTRON AND PREPARE IT FOR MY RETURN. DO YOU UNDERSTAND?
BUT HOW WILL YOU FIND IT WITHOUT MY HEL—
DO YOU NDERSTAND?!
YEEAARGH!
Y-YES!
AT THE SHIP'S COMPLETION, GATHER THE CREW. YOUR DECEPTICON FORCES HAVE GROWN IN IMPRESSIVE NUMBERS, MEGATRON. THESE FORCES WILL DO WELL ON MY JOURNEY.
CONTINUE TO HUNT DOWN ANY DEFECTORS AND ELIMINATE THEM, MEGATRON.
WE SHALL. THEY HAVE SCATTERED TO OTHER REGIONS OF THE PLANET. OUR SOLDIERS ARE IN PURSUIT. THEY WILL PAY FOR LEAVING OUR SIDE.
SCATTERED? DOES THIS NOT MAKE YOU LEERY? ASK YOURSELF THIS, IF THEY DO NOT WISH TO SIDE WITH THE MOST POWERFUL ARMY ON THE PLANET AND IN THE GALAXY...

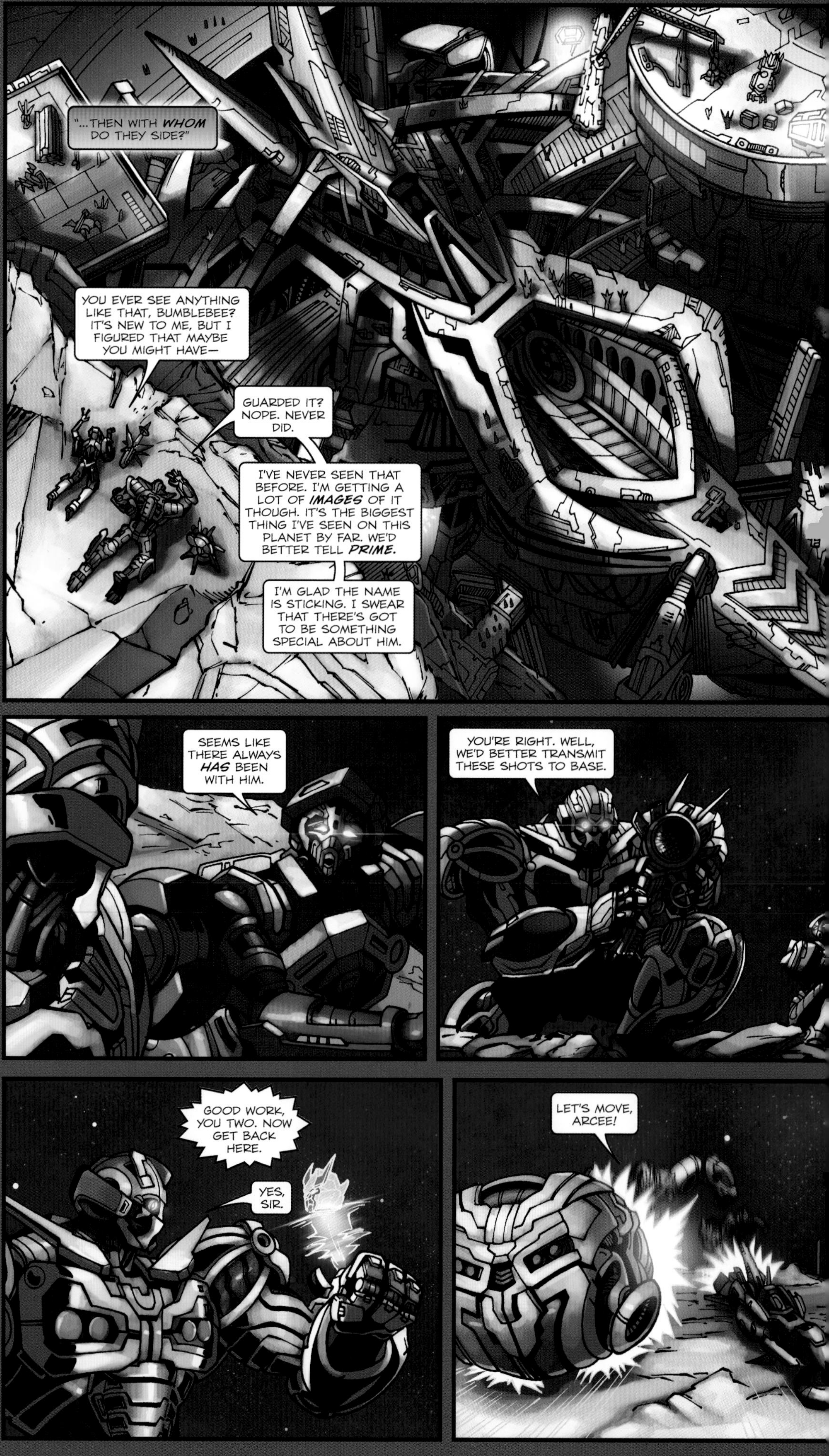
"...THEN WITH WHOM DO THEY SIDE?"
YOU EVER SEE ANYTHING LIKE THAT, BUMBLEBEE? IT'S NEW TO ME, BUT I FIGURED THAT MAYBE YOU MIGHT HAVE—
GUARDED IT? NOPE. NEVER DID.
I'VE NEVER SEEN THAT BEFORE. I'M GETTING A LOT OF IMAGES OF IT THOUGH. IT'S THE BIGGEST THING I'VE SEEN ON THIS PLANET BY FAR. WE'D BETTER TELL PRIME.
I'M GLAD THE NAME IS STICKING. I SWEAR THAT THERE'S GOT TO BE SOMETHING SPECIAL ABOUT HIM.
SEEMS LIKE THERE ALWAYS HAS BEEN WITH HIM.
YOU'RE RIGHT. WELL, WE'D BETTER TRANSMIT THESE SHOTS TO BASE.
GOOD WORK, YOU TWO. NOW GET BACK HERE.
YES, SIR.
LET'S MOVE, ARCEE!

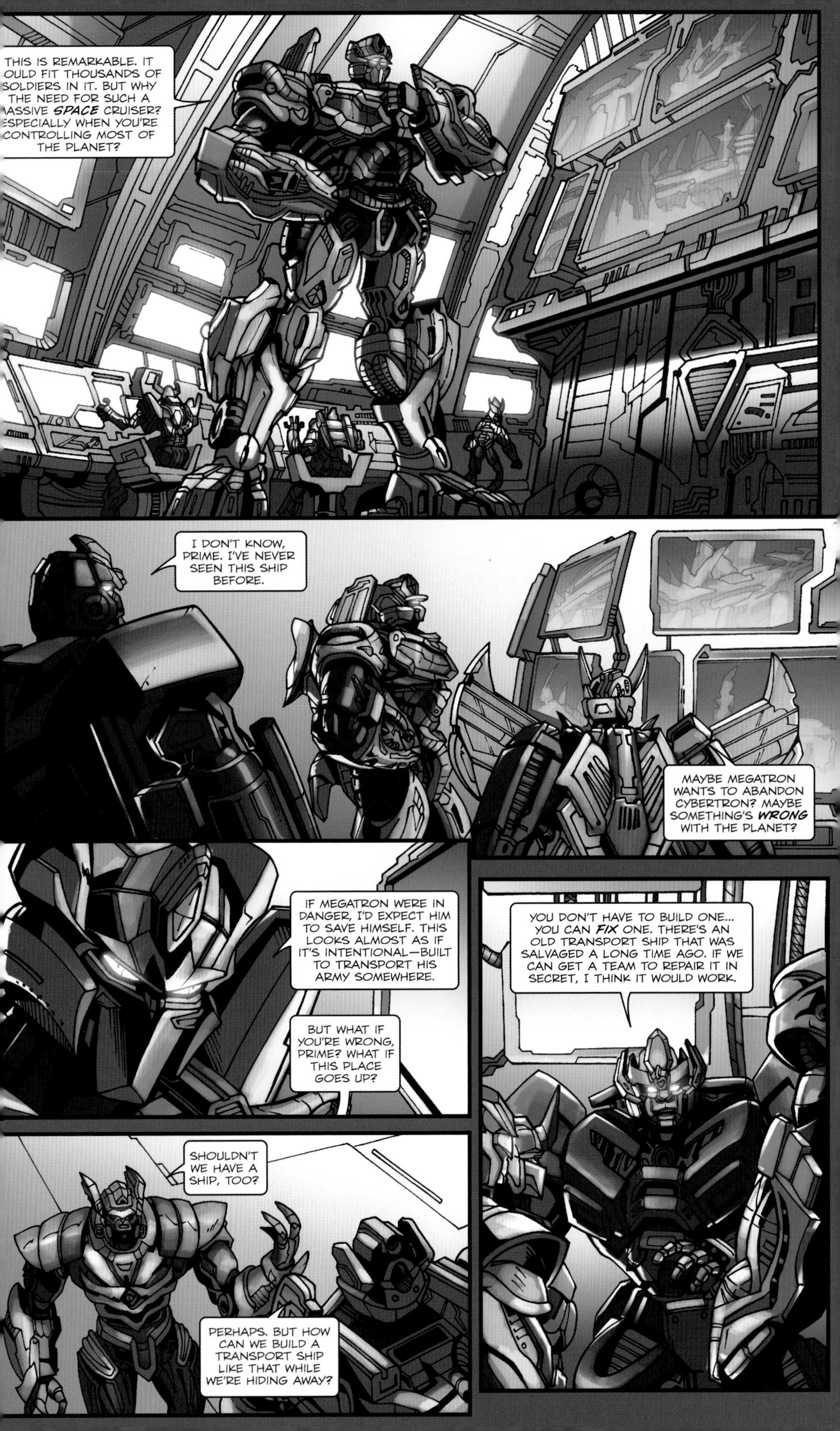
THIS IS REMARKABLE. IT
OULD FIT THOUSANDS OF
SOLDIERS IN IT. BUT WHY
THE NEED FOR SUCH A
ASSIVE SPACE CRUISER?
SPECIALLY WHEN YOU'RE
CONTROLLING MOST OF
THE PLANET?
I DON'T KNOW, PRIME. I'VE NEVER SEEN THIS SHIP BEFORE.
MAYBE MEGATRON WANTS TO ABANDON CYBERTRON? MAYBE SOMETHING'S WRONG WITH THE PLANET?
IF MEGATRON WERE IN DANGER, I'D EXPECT HIM TO SAVE HIMSELF. THIS LOOKS ALMOST AS IF IT'S INTENTIONAL—BUILT TO TRANSPORT HIS ARMY SOMEWHERE.
BUT WHAT IF YOU'RE WRONG, PRIME? WHAT IF THIS PLACE GOES UP?
SHOULDN'T WE HAVE A SHIP, TOO?
PERHAPS. BUT HOW CAN WE BUILD A TRANSPORT SHIP LIKE THAT WHILE WE'RE HIDING AWAY?
YOU DON'T HAVE TO BUILD ONE... YOU CAN FIX ONE. THERE'S AN OLD TRANSPORT SHIP THAT WAS SALVAGED A LONG TIME AGO. IF WE CAN GET A TEAM TO REPAIR IT IN SECRET, I THINK IT WOULD WORK.

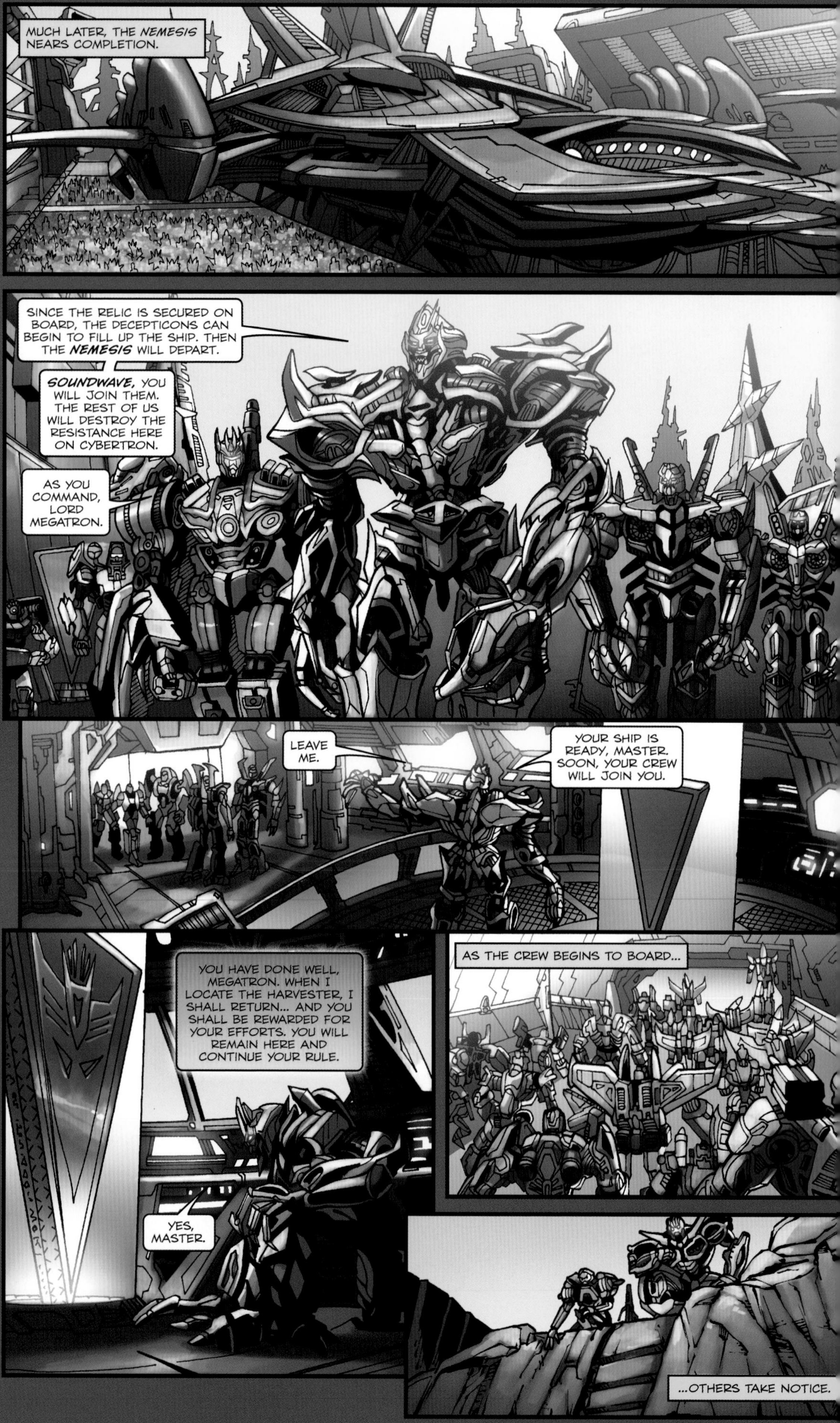

MUCH LATER, THE *NEMESIS* NEARS COMPLETION.
SINCE THE RELIC IS SECURED ON BOARD, THE DECEPTICONS CAN BEGIN TO FILL UP THE SHIP. THEN THE ***NEMESIS*** WILL DEPART.
SOUNDWAVE, YOU WILL JOIN THEM. THE REST OF US WILL DESTROY THE RESISTANCE HERE ON CYBERTRON.
AS YOU COMMAND, LORD MEGATRON.
LEAVE ME.
YOUR SHIP IS READY, MASTER. SOON, YOUR CREW WILL JOIN YOU.
YOU HAVE DONE WELL, MEGATRON. WHEN I LOCATE THE HARVESTER, I SHALL RETURN... AND YOU SHALL BE REWARDED FOR YOUR EFFORTS. YOU WILL REMAIN HERE AND CONTINUE YOUR RULE.
YES, MASTER.
AS THE CREW BEGINS TO BOARD...
...OTHERS TAKE NOTICE.

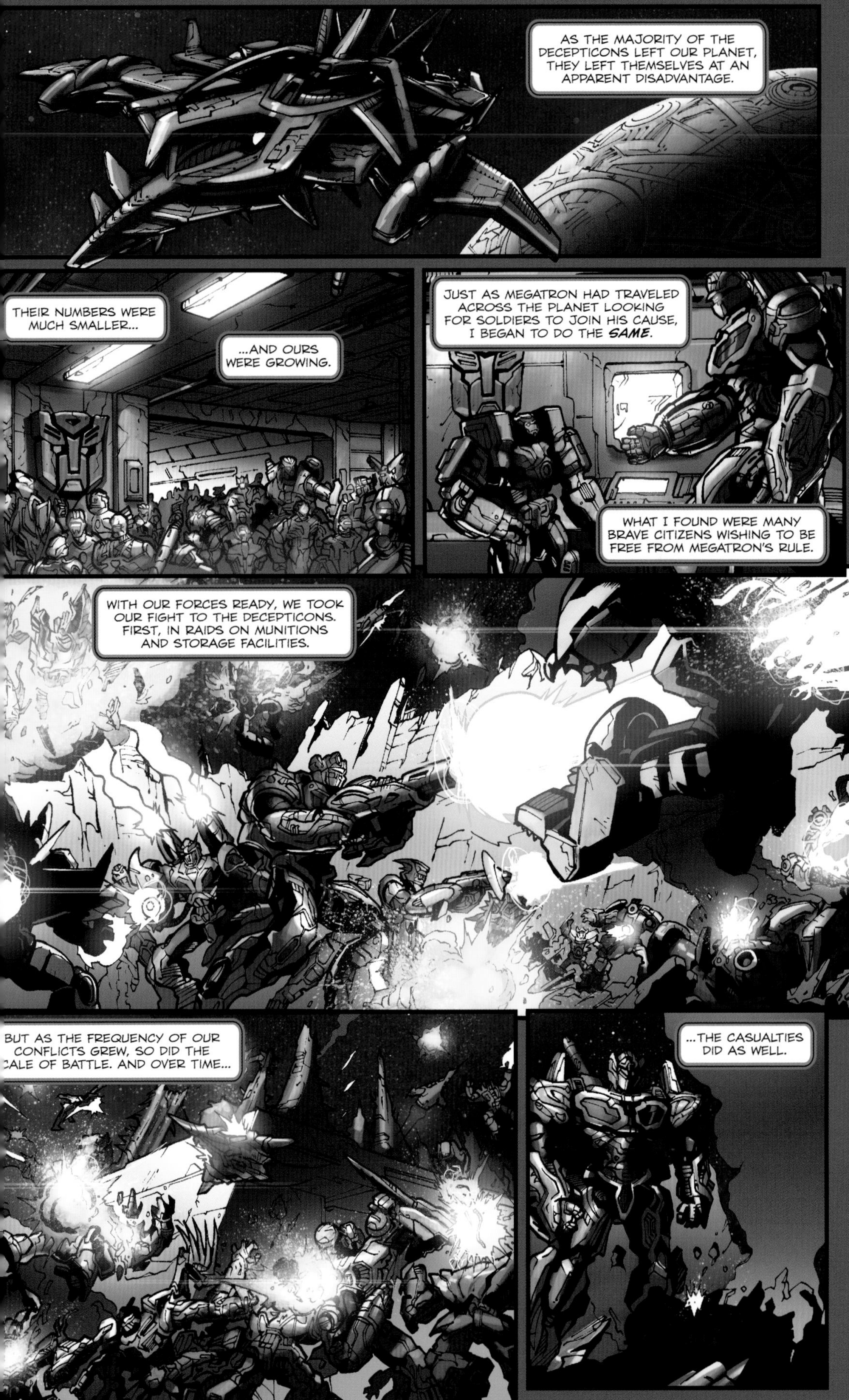
AS THE MAJORITY OF THE DECEPTICONS LEFT OUR PLANET, THEY LEFT THEMSELVES AT AN APPARENT DISADVANTAGE.
THEIR NUMBERS WERE MUCH SMALLER...
...AND OURS WERE GROWING.
JUST AS MEGATRON HAD TRAVELED ACROSS THE PLANET LOOKING FOR SOLDIERS TO JOIN HIS CAUSE, I BEGAN TO DO THE *SAME*.
WHAT I FOUND WERE MANY BRAVE CITIZENS WISHING TO BE FREE FROM MEGATRON'S RULE.
WITH OUR FORCES READY, WE TOOK OUR FIGHT TO THE DECEPTICONS. FIRST, IN RAIDS ON MUNITIONS AND STORAGE FACILITIES.
BUT AS THE FREQUENCY OF OUR CONFLICTS GREW, SO DID THE CALE OF BATTLE. AND OVER TIME...
...THE CASUALTIES DID AS WELL.

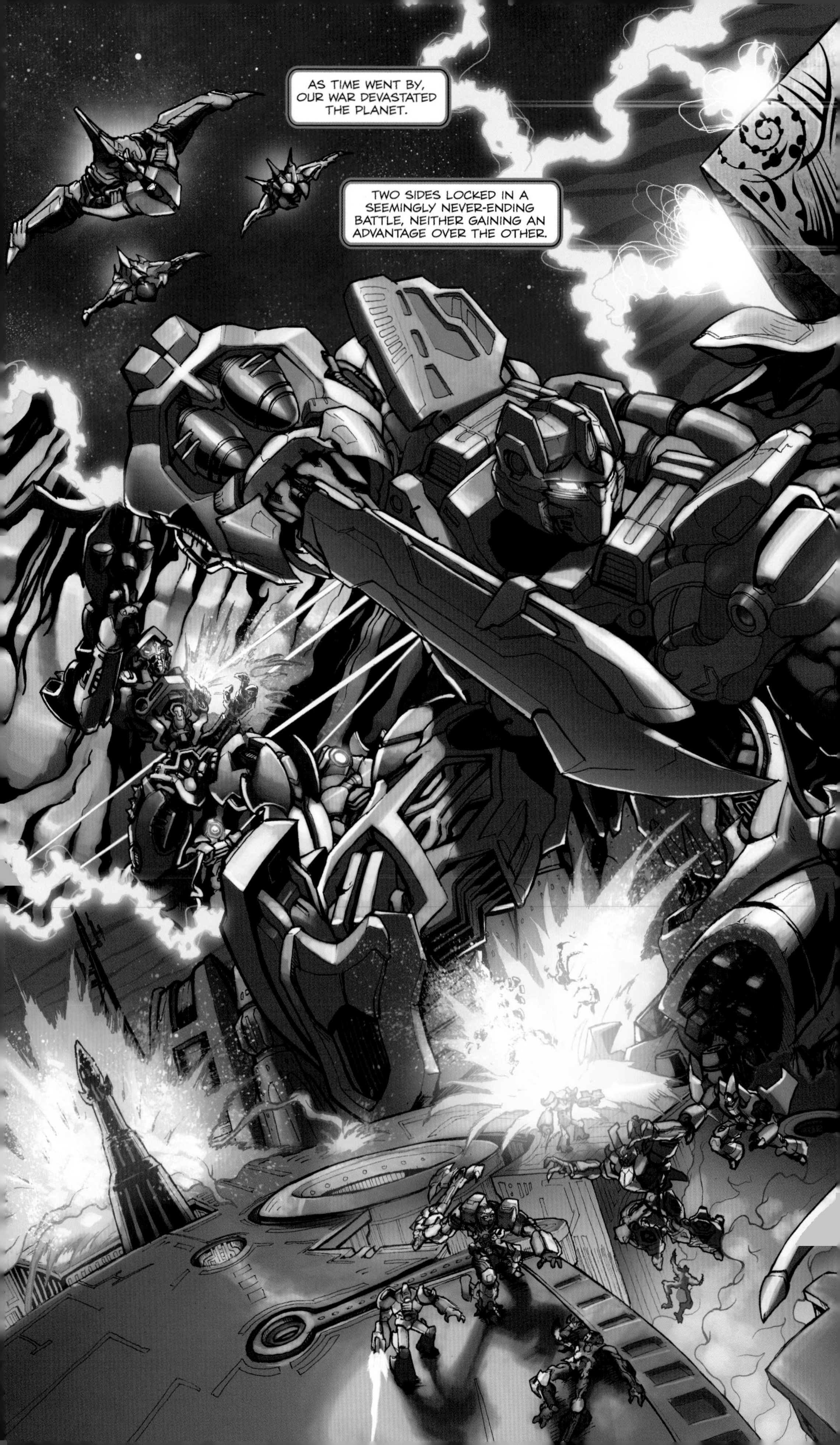
AS TIME WENT BY, OUR WAR DEVASTATED THE PLANET.
TWO SIDES LOCKED IN A SEEMINGLY NEVER-ENDING BATTLE, NEITHER GAINING AN ADVANTAGE OVER THE OTHER.

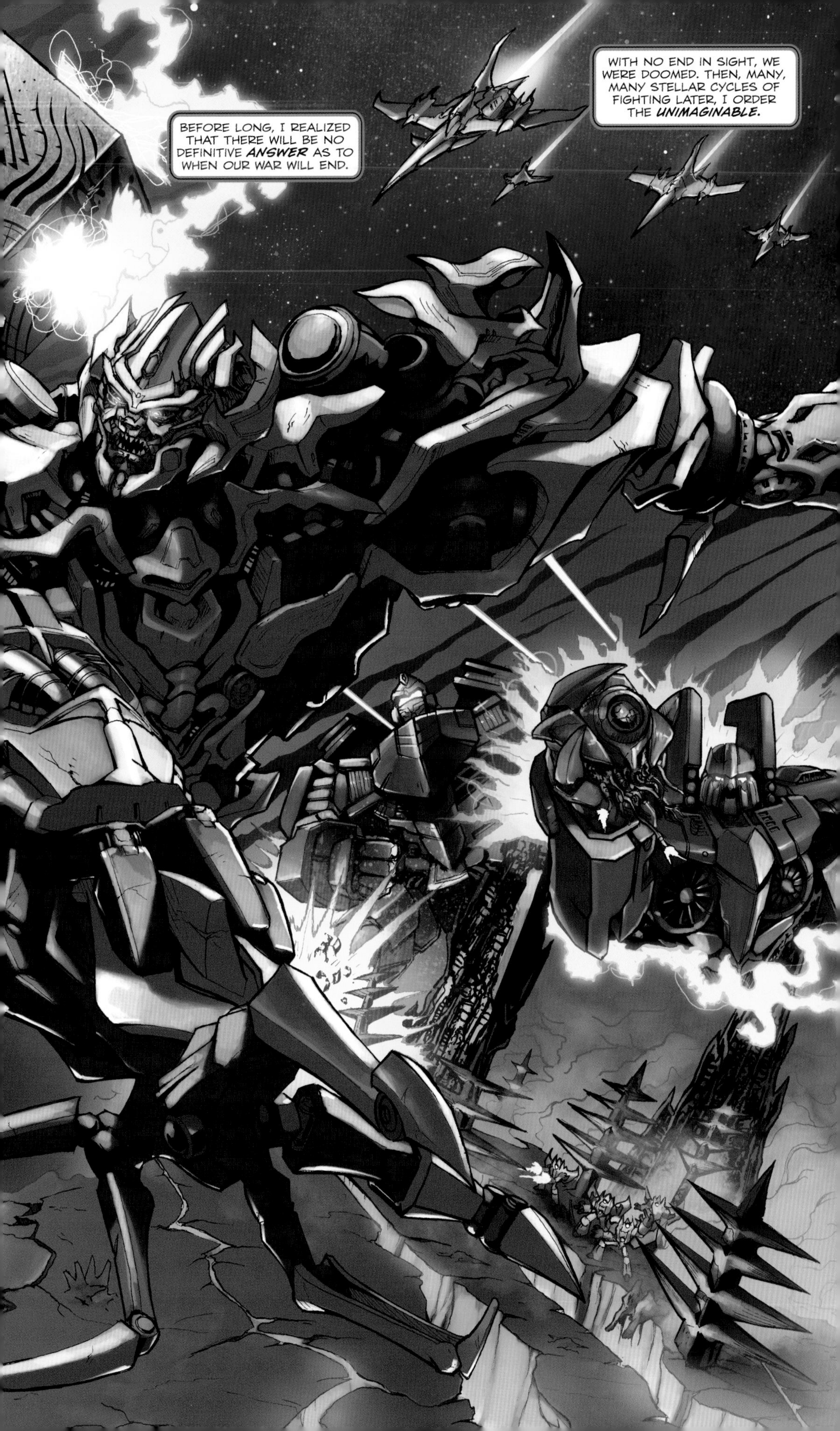
BEFORE LONG, I REALIZED THAT THERE WILL BE NO DEFINITIVE ANSWER AS TO WHEN OUR WAR WILL END.
WITH NO END IN SIGHT, WE WERE DOOMED. THEN, MANY, MANY STELLAR CYCLES OF FIGHTING LATER, I ORDER THE UNIMAGINABLE.

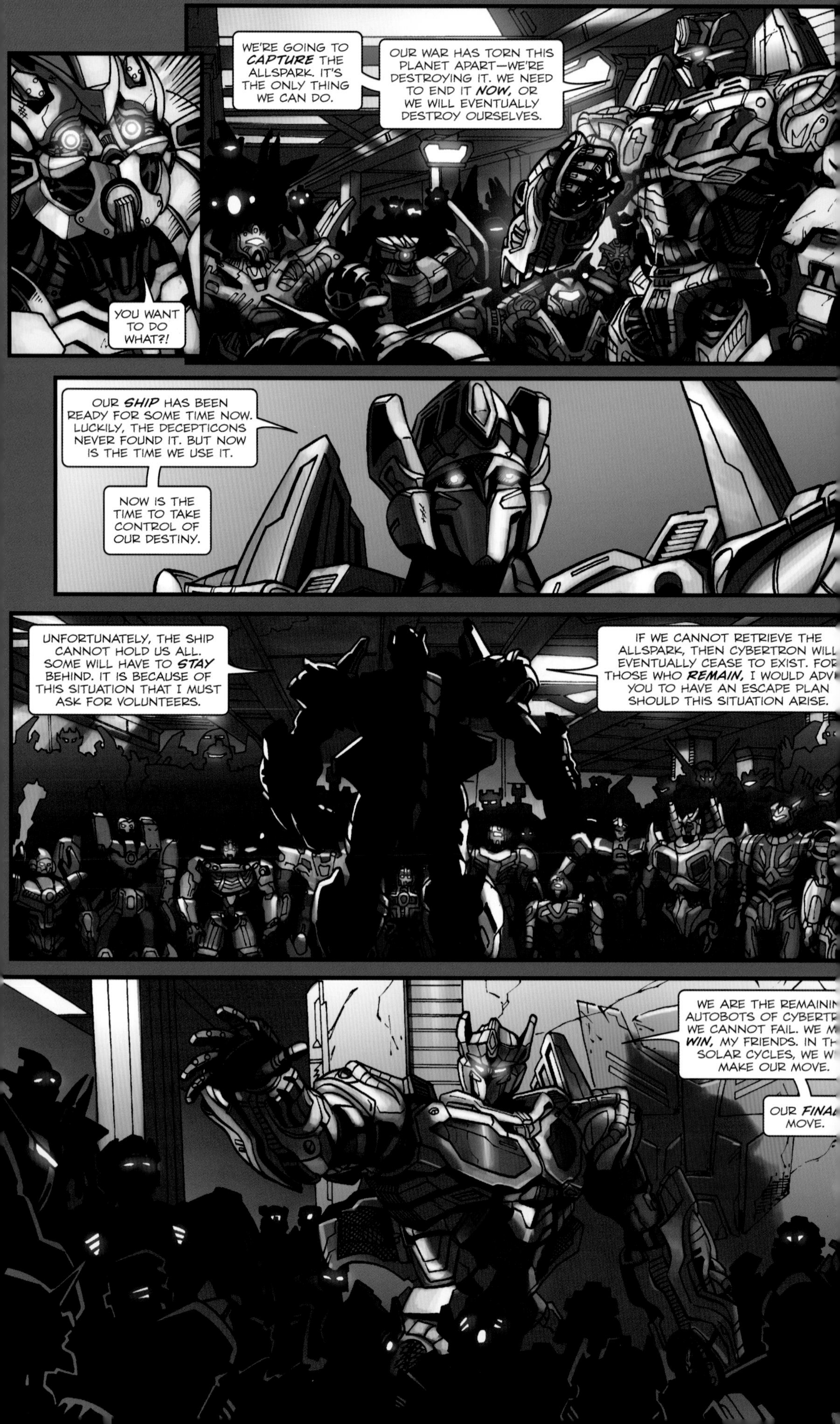
WE'RE GOING TO CAPTURE THE ALLSPARK. IT'S THE ONLY THING WE CAN DO.
OUR WAR HAS TORN THIS PLANET APART—WE'RE DESTROYING IT. WE NEED TO END IT NOW, OR WE WILL EVENTUALLY DESTROY OURSELVES.
YOU WANT TO DO WHAT?!
OUR SHIP HAS BEEN READY FOR SOME TIME NOW. LUCKILY, THE DECEPTICONS NEVER FOUND IT. BUT NOW IS THE TIME WE USE IT.
NOW IS THE TIME TO TAKE CONTROL OF OUR DESTINY.
UNFORTUNATELY, THE SHIP CANNOT HOLD US ALL. SOME WILL HAVE TO STAY BEHIND. IT IS BECAUSE OF THIS SITUATION THAT I MUST ASK FOR VOLUNTEERS.
IF WE CANNOT RETRIEVE THE ALLSPARK, THEN CYBERTRON WILL EVENTUALLY CEASE TO EXIST. FOR THOSE WHO REMAIN, I WOULD ADV YOU TO HAVE AN ESCAPE PLAN SHOULD THIS SITUATION ARISE.
WE ARE THE REMAININ AUTOBOTS OF CYBERTR WE CANNOT FAIL. WE M WIN, MY FRIENDS. IN TH SOLAR CYCLES, WE W MAKE OUR MOVE.
OUR FINA MOVE.

FEW OF THEM KNEW WHAT I HAD *PLANNED* TO DO. ALL THEY UNDERSTOOD WAS THAT WE WERE TAKING THE ALLSPARK AND SOMEHOW BRINGING IT WITH US ON THE SHIP.

BUT THAT WOULD LEAVE *LESS* ROOM FOR SOME OF US, ROOM THAT I WOULD RATHER FILL WITH MORE SURVIVORS OF THIS WAR. REFUGEES LEFT WITH NOWHERE TO GO. I HAD OTHER PLANS.

TIMING WAS CRUCIAL, AND *HIDING* IT WAS A TWISTED GAME WE HAD PLAYED FOR FAR TOO LONG. UNABLE TO REACH A SOLUTION TO THE PROBLEM, I SOON GAVE WHAT WOULD BE MY *LAST* ORDERS ON CYBERTRON.

WHILE ONE TEAM FOUGHT AT THE *TEMPLE*...

...A BRAVE FEW FOUGHT IN *TYGER PAX*. BOTH TEAMS SUFFERED LOSSES, BUT ULTIMATELY THE PLAN WORKED...

...AND THE ALLSPARK WAS SENT INTO SPACE.

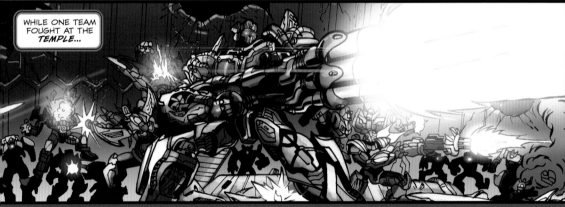

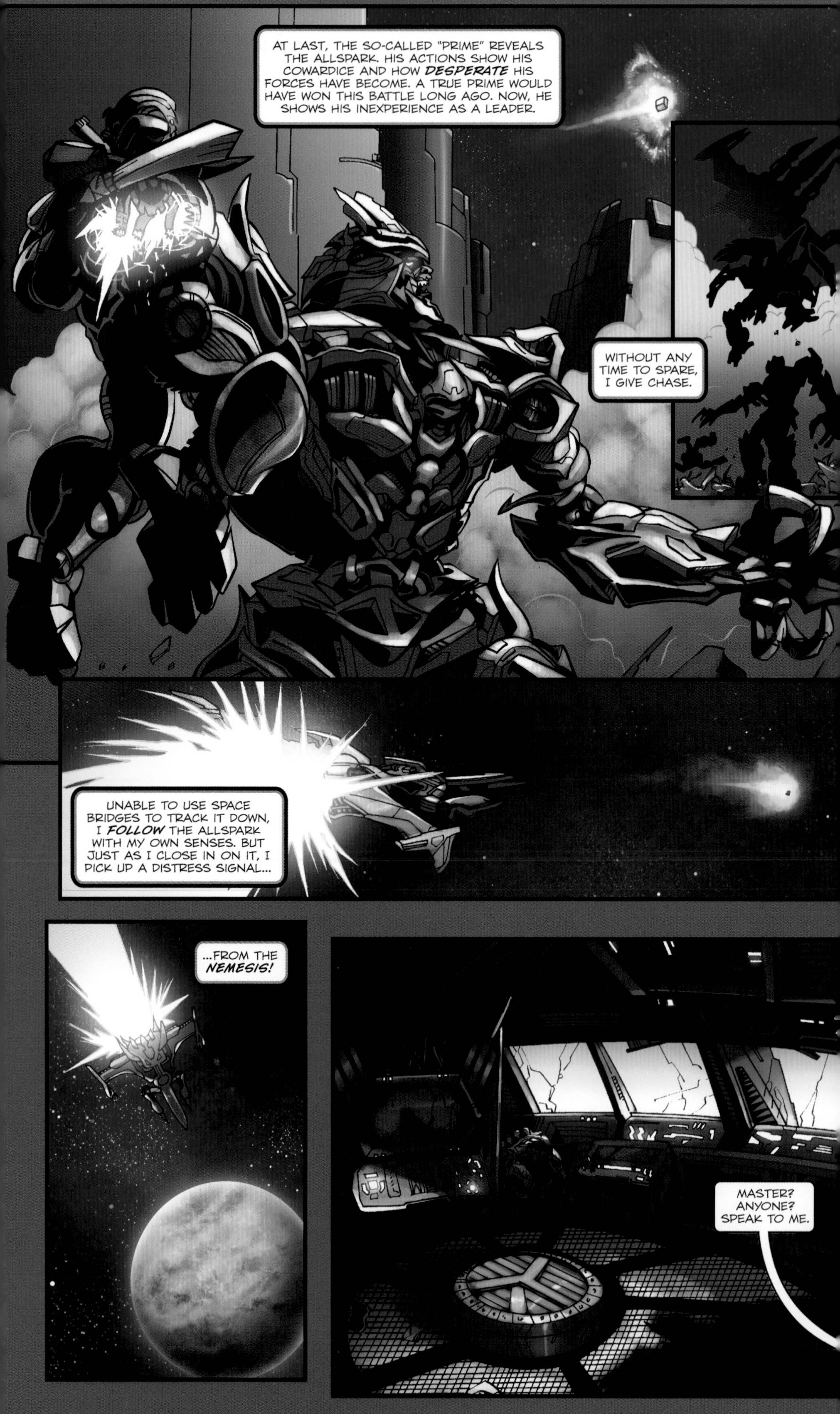
AT LAST, THE SO-CALLED "PRIME" REVEALS THE ALLSPARK. HIS ACTIONS SHOW HIS COWARDICE AND HOW DESPERATE HIS FORCES HAVE BECOME. A TRUE PRIME WOULD HAVE WON THIS BATTLE LONG AGO. NOW, HE SHOWS HIS INEXPERIENCE AS A LEADER.
WITHOUT ANY TIME TO SPARE, I GIVE CHASE.
UNABLE TO USE SPACE BRIDGES TO TRACK IT DOWN, I FOLLOW THE ALLSPARK WITH MY OWN SENSES. BUT JUST AS I CLOSE IN ON IT, I PICK UP A DISTRESS SIGNAL...
...FROM THE NEMESIS!
MASTER? ANYONE? SPEAK TO ME.

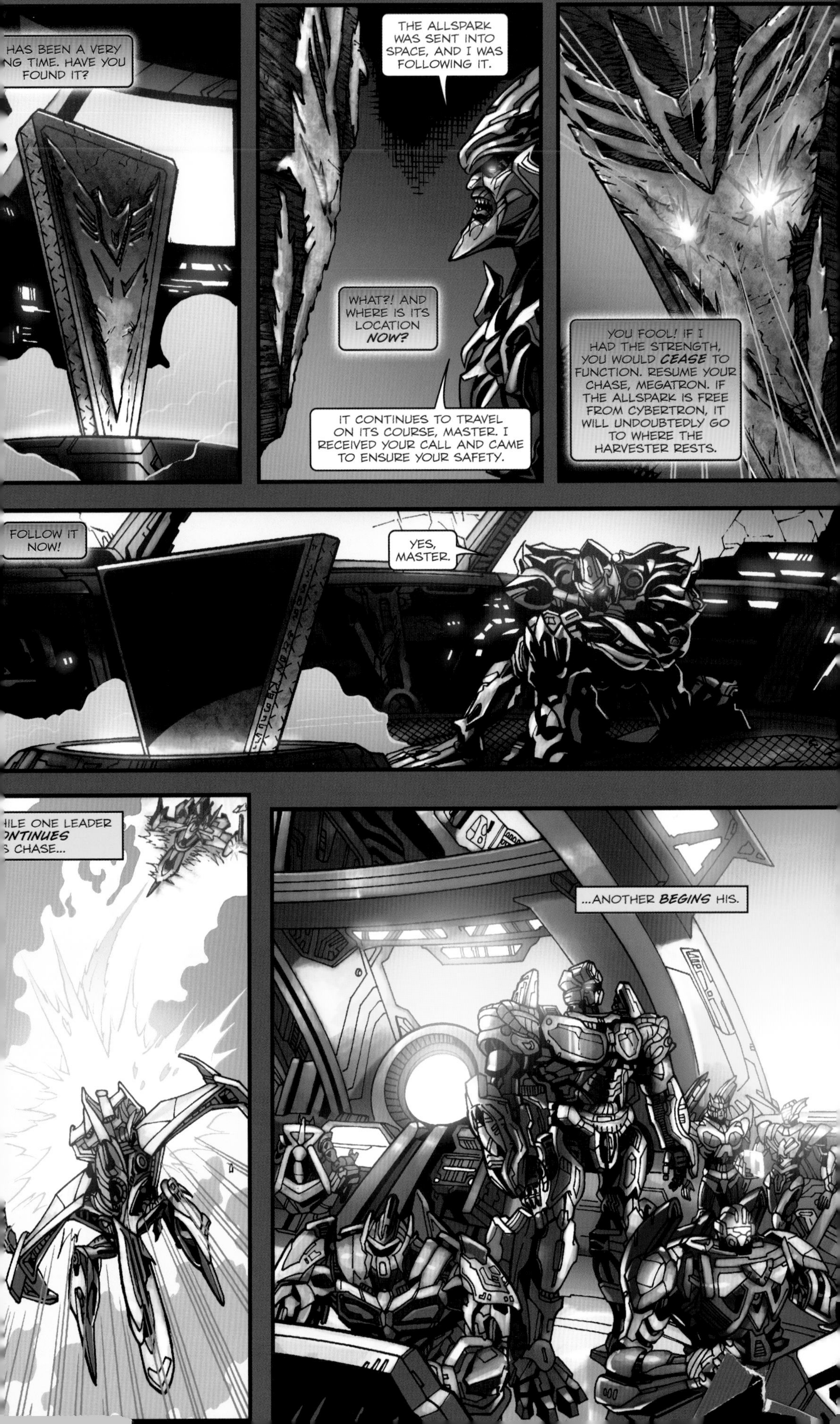
HAS BEEN A VERY
NG TIME. HAVE YOU FOUND IT?
THE ALLSPARK WAS SENT INTO SPACE, AND I WAS FOLLOWING IT.
WHAT?! AND WHERE IS ITS LOCATION NOW?
IT CONTINUES TO TRAVEL ON ITS COURSE, MASTER. I RECEIVED YOUR CALL AND CAME TO ENSURE YOUR SAFETY.
YOU FOOL! IF I HAD THE STRENGTH, YOU WOULD CEASE TO FUNCTION. RESUME YOUR CHASE, MEGATRON. IF THE ALLSPARK IS FREE FROM CYBERTRON, IT WILL UNDOUBTEDLY GO TO WHERE THE HARVESTER RESTS.
FOLLOW IT NOW!
YES, MASTER.
HILE ONE LEADER
ONTINUES
S CHASE...
...ANOTHER BEGINS HIS.

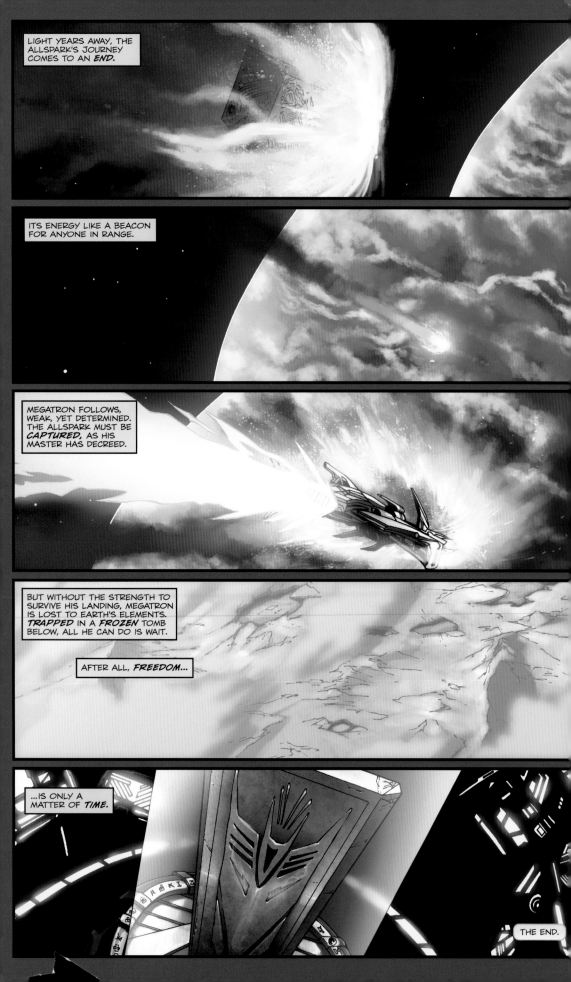

LIGHT YEARS AWAY, THE ALLSPARK'S JOURNEY COMES TO AN *END.*

ITS ENERGY LIKE A BEACON FOR ANYONE IN RANGE.

MEGATRON FOLLOWS, WEAK, YET DETERMINED. THE ALLSPARK MUST BE *CAPTURED,* AS HIS MASTER HAS DECREED.

BUT WITHOUT THE STRENGTH TO SURVIVE HIS LANDING, MEGATRON IS LOST TO EARTH'S ELEMENTS. *TRAPPED* IN A *FROZEN* TOMB BELOW, ALL HE CAN DO IS WAIT.

AFTER ALL, *FREEDOM...*

...IS ONLY A MATTER OF *TIME.*

THE END.

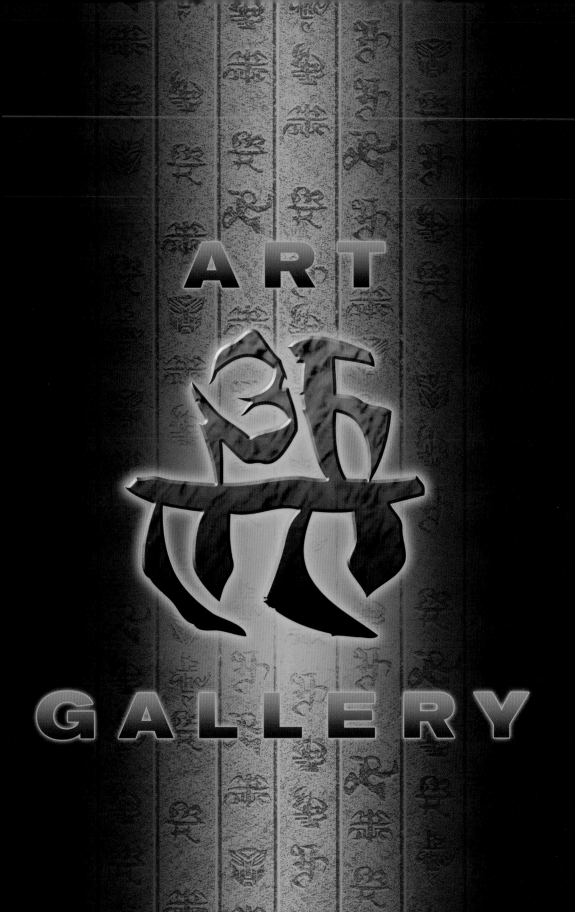

ART

GALLERY

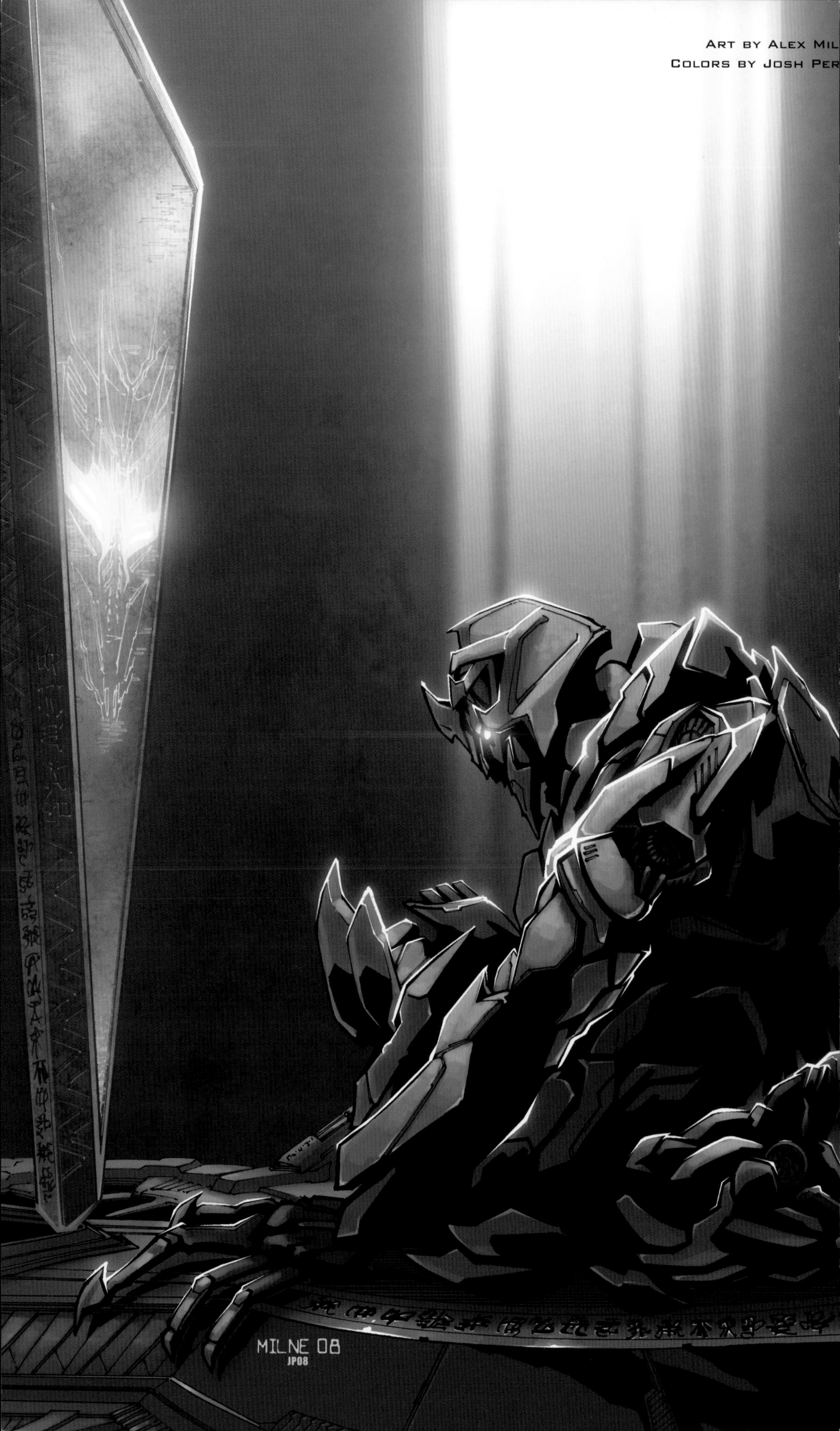
Art by Alex Mil
Colors by Josh Per
MILNE 08
JP08

by Josh Nizzi

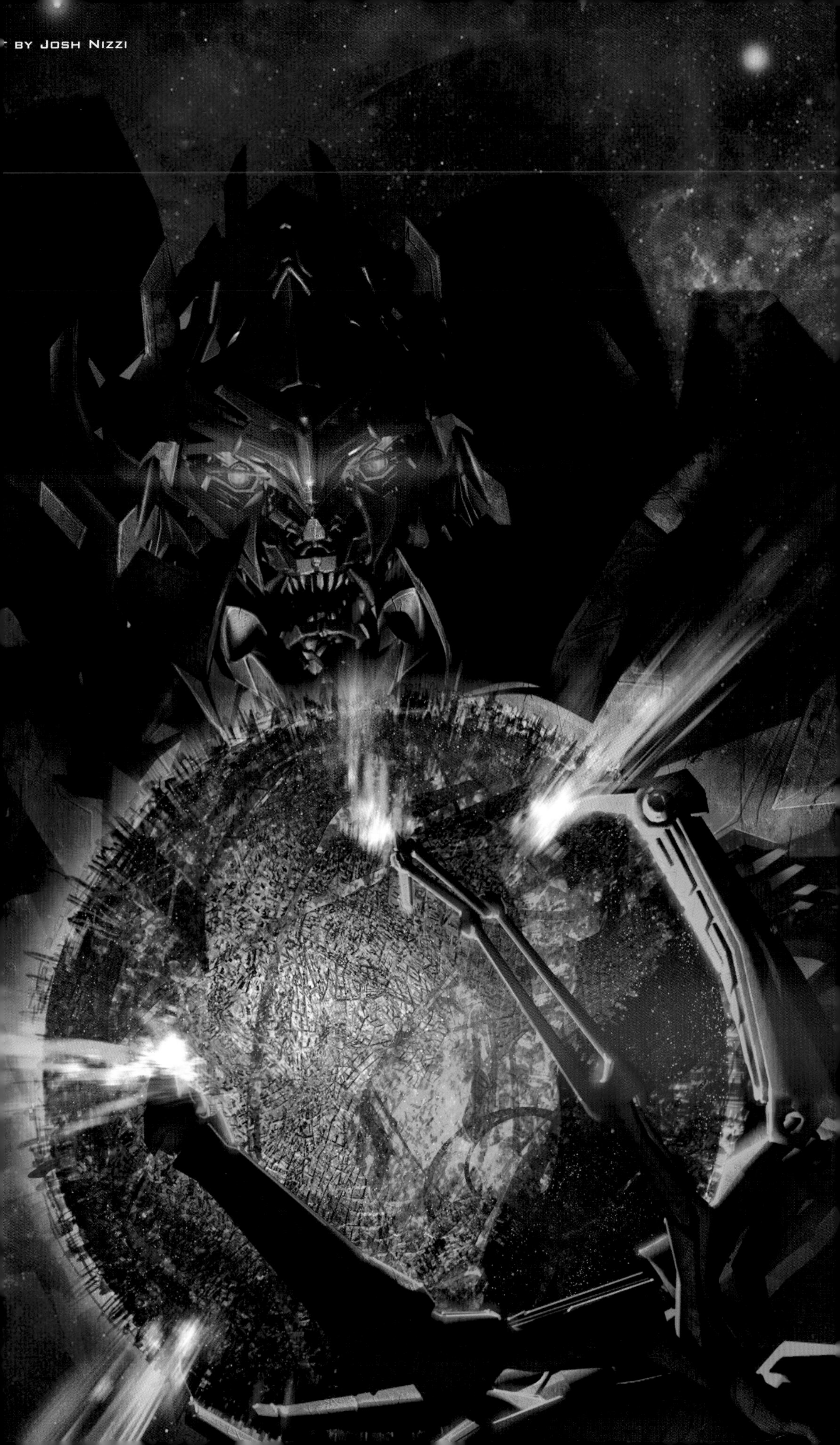

Art by Alex Milne
Colors by Joana Lafuente

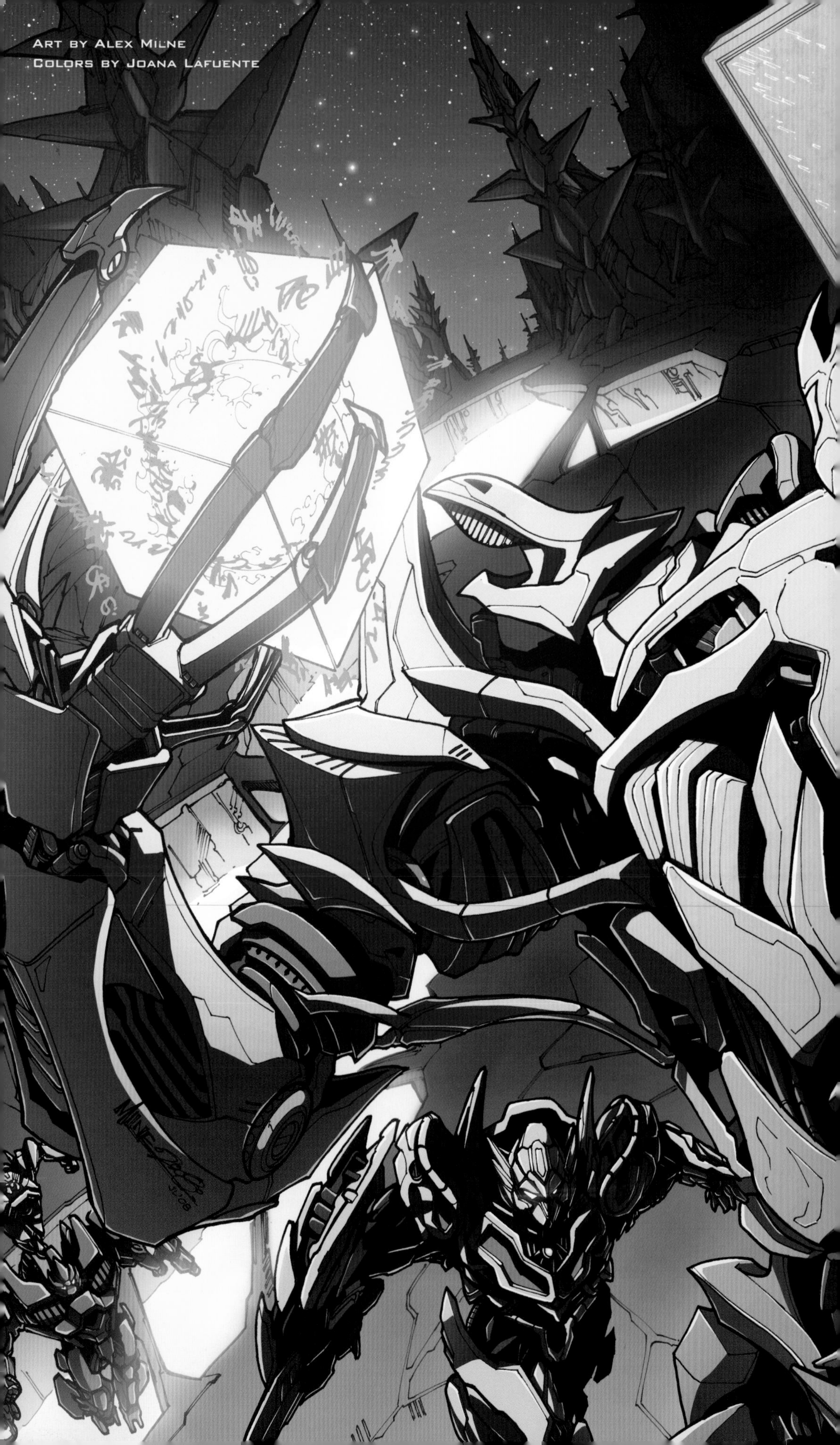

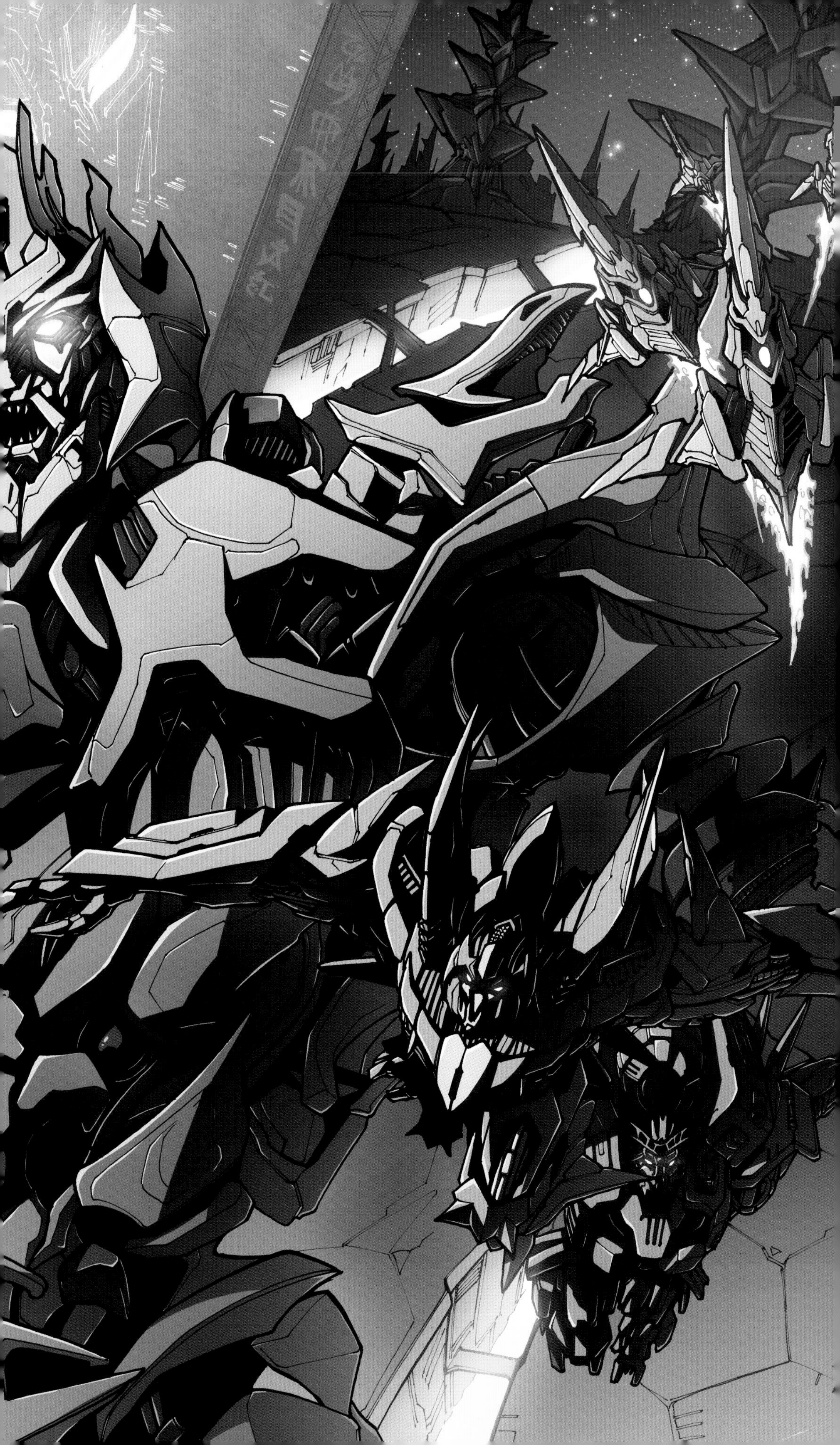

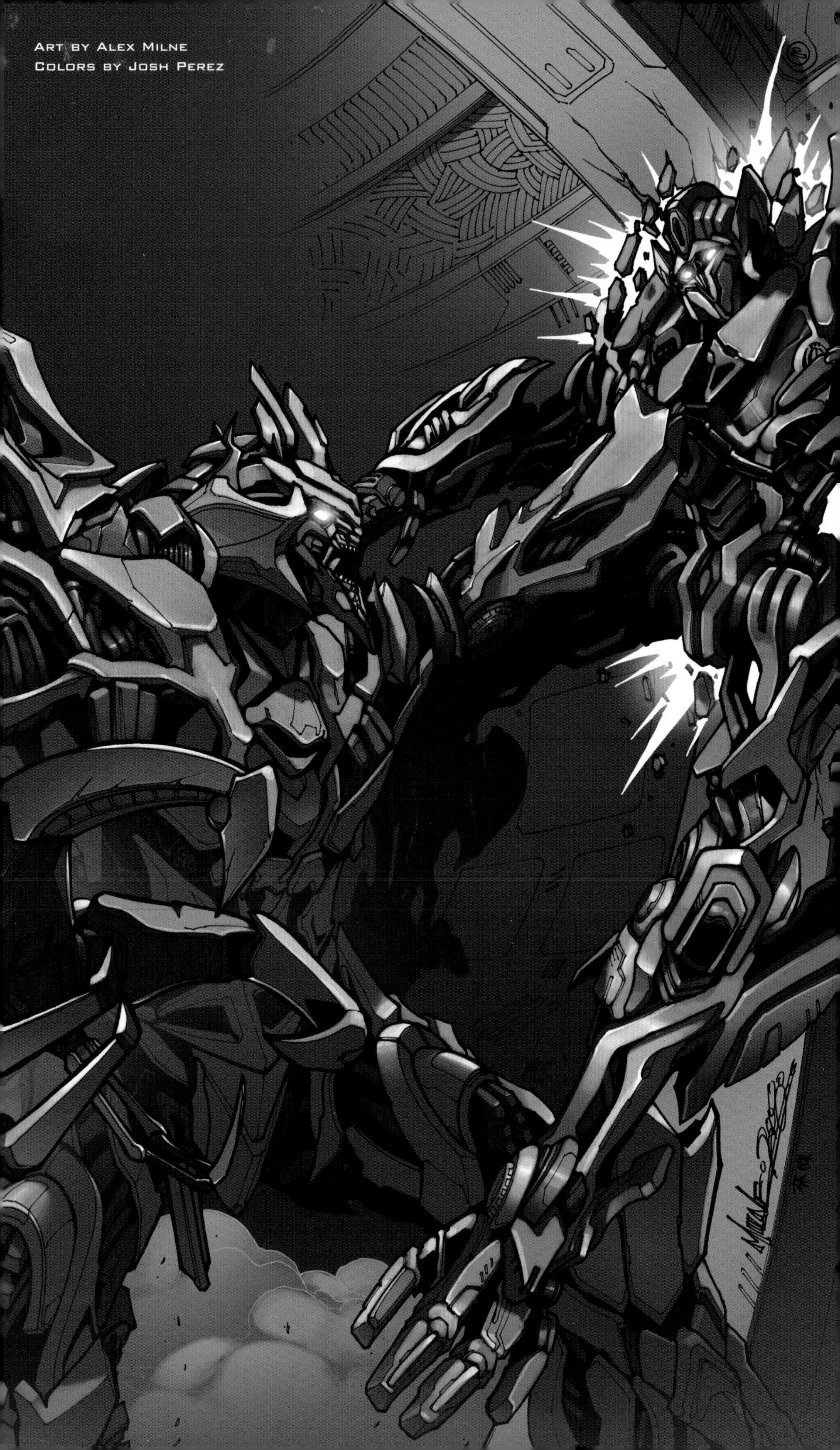

Art by Alex Milne
Colors by Josh Perez

Art by Josh Nizzi

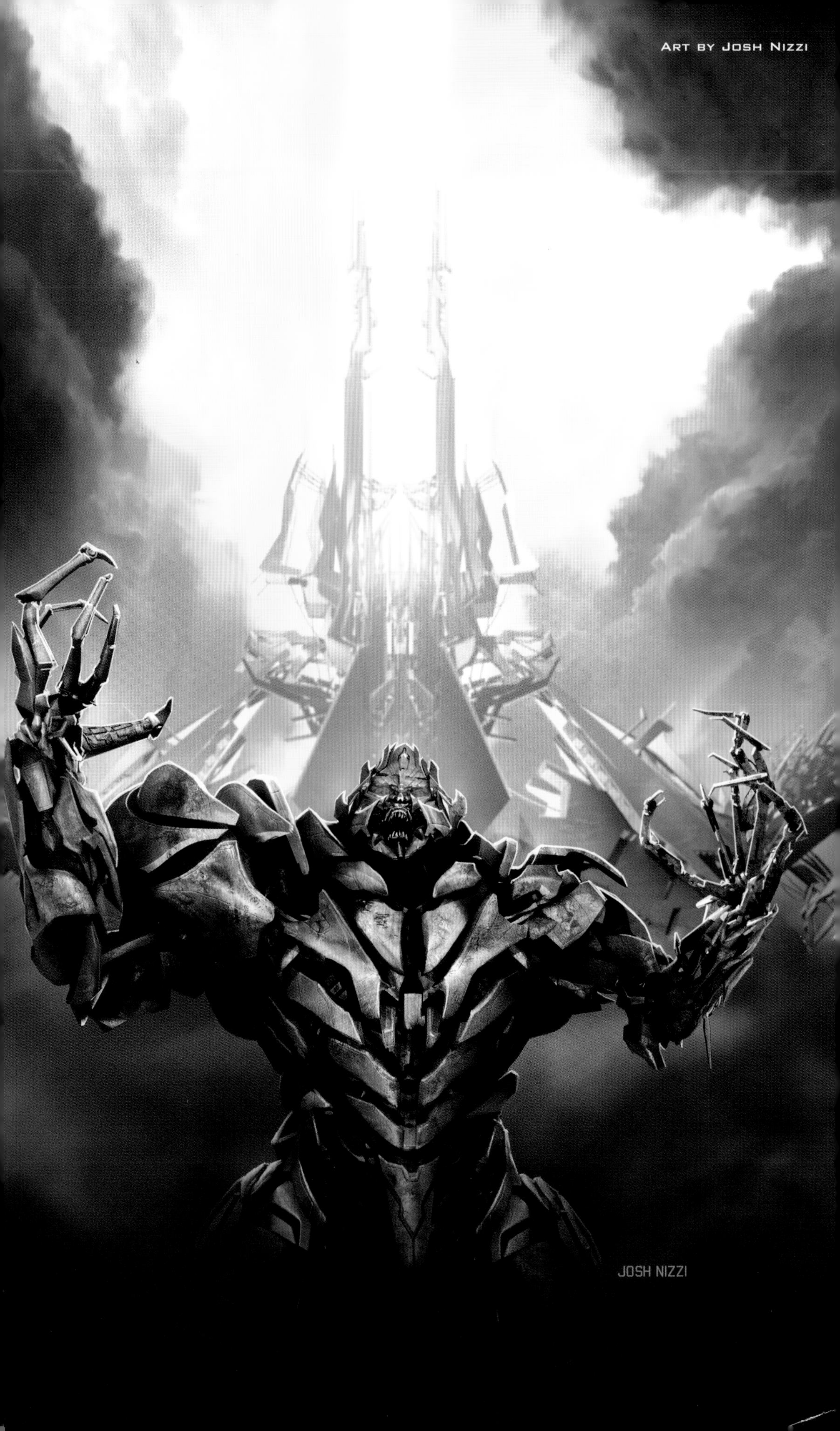
JOSH NIZZI

ART BY DON FIGUER
COLORS BY JOSH PE

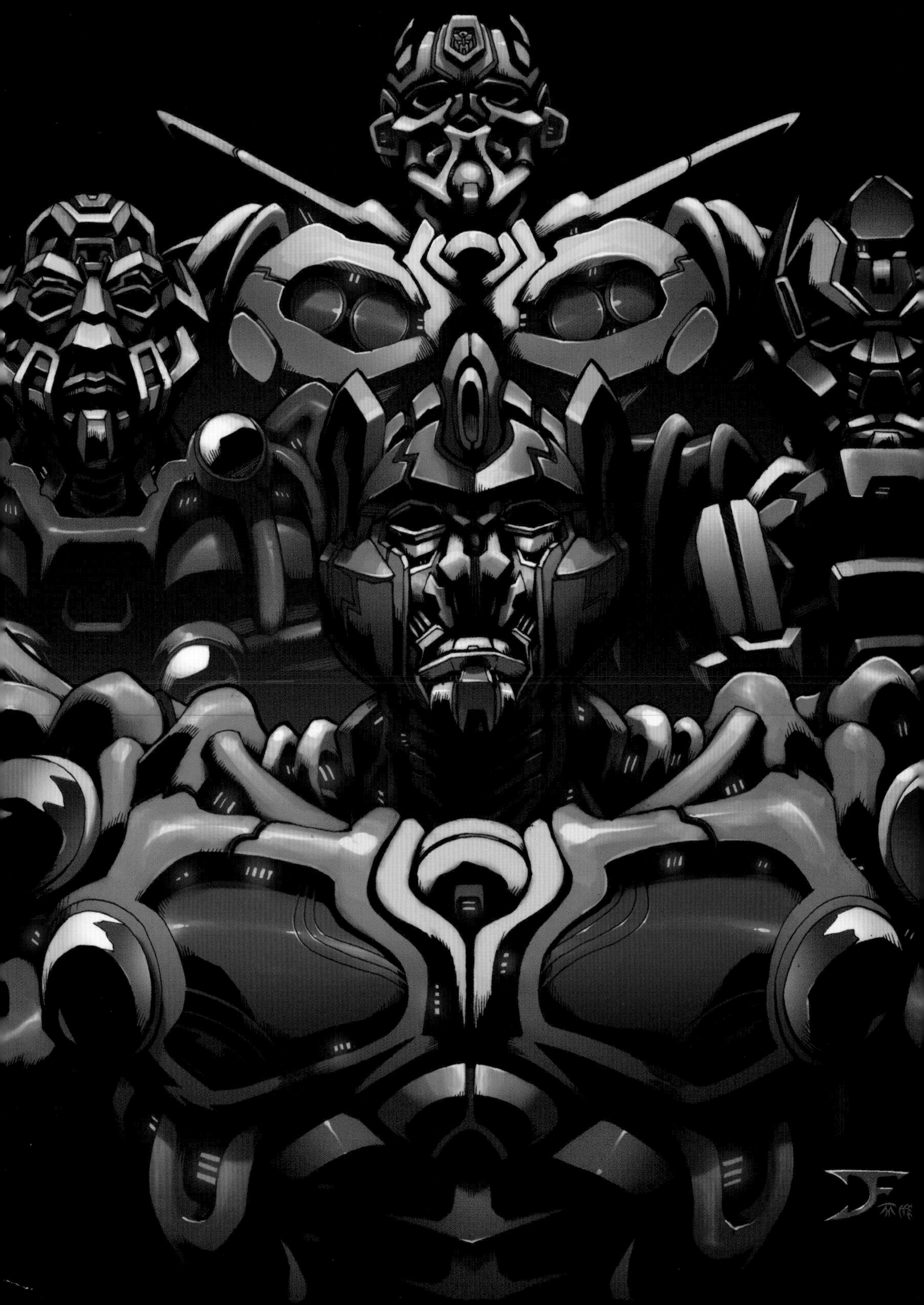

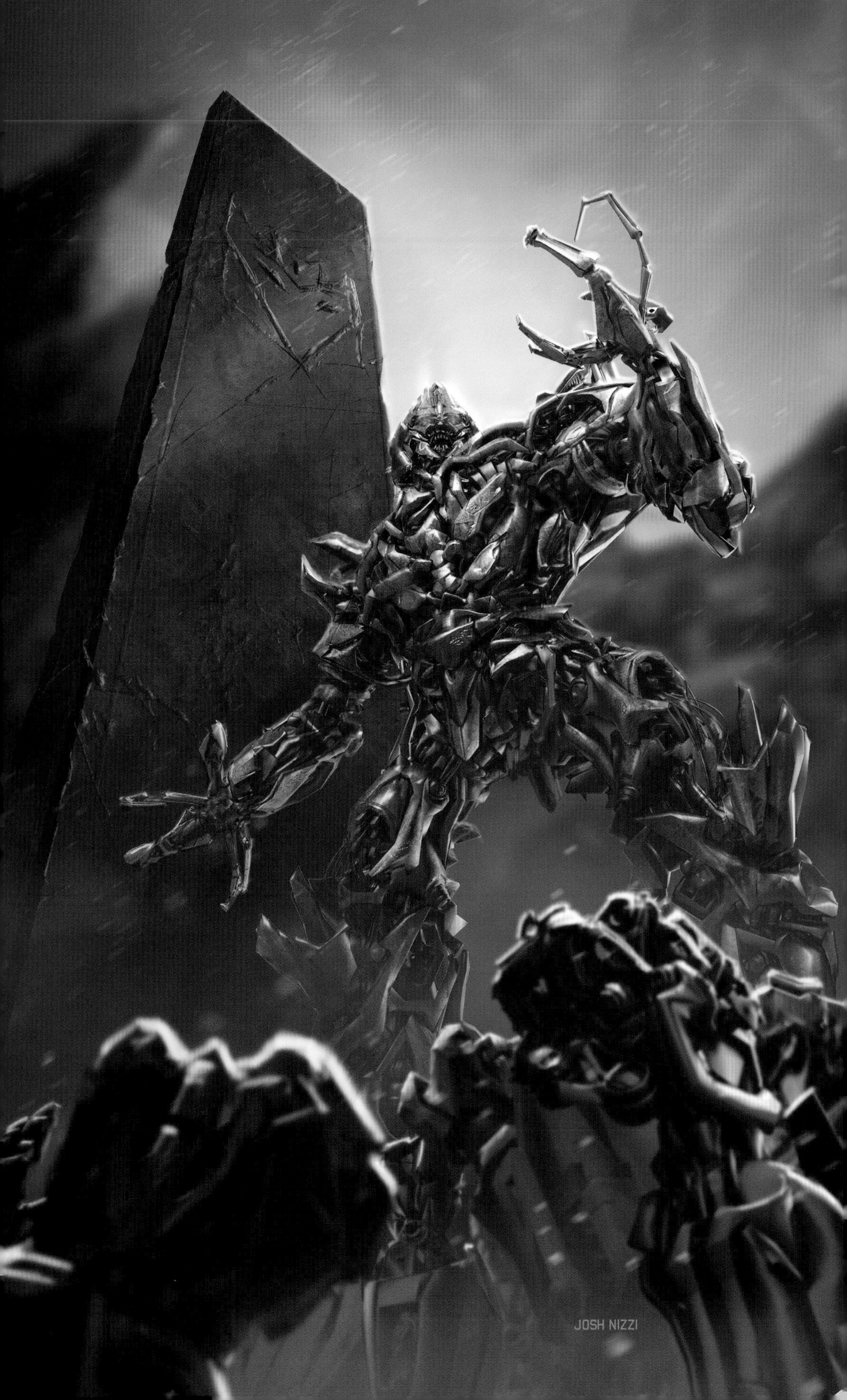
JOSH NIZZI

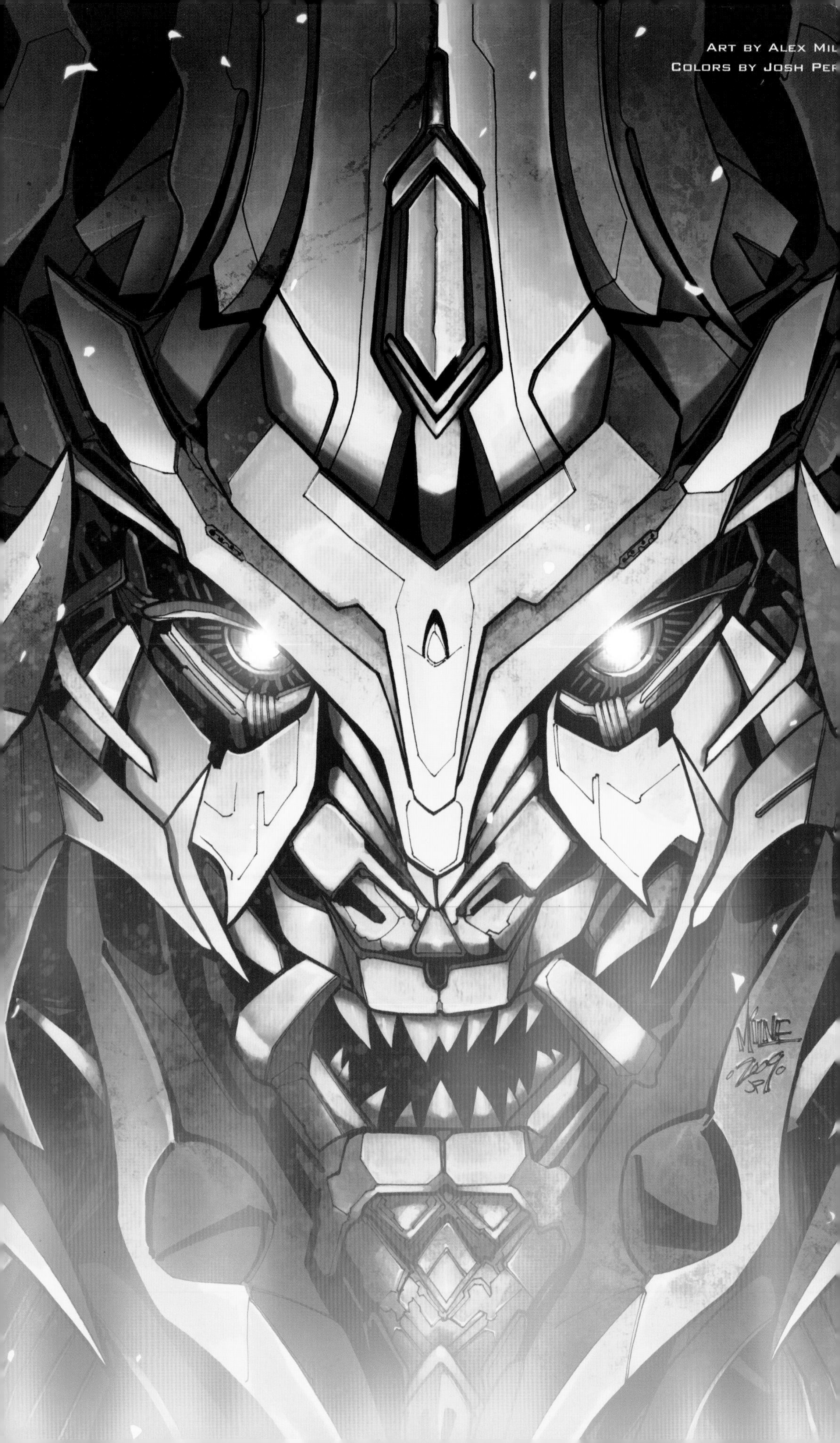
Art by Alex Mil
Colors by Josh Per

T BY JOSH NIZZI

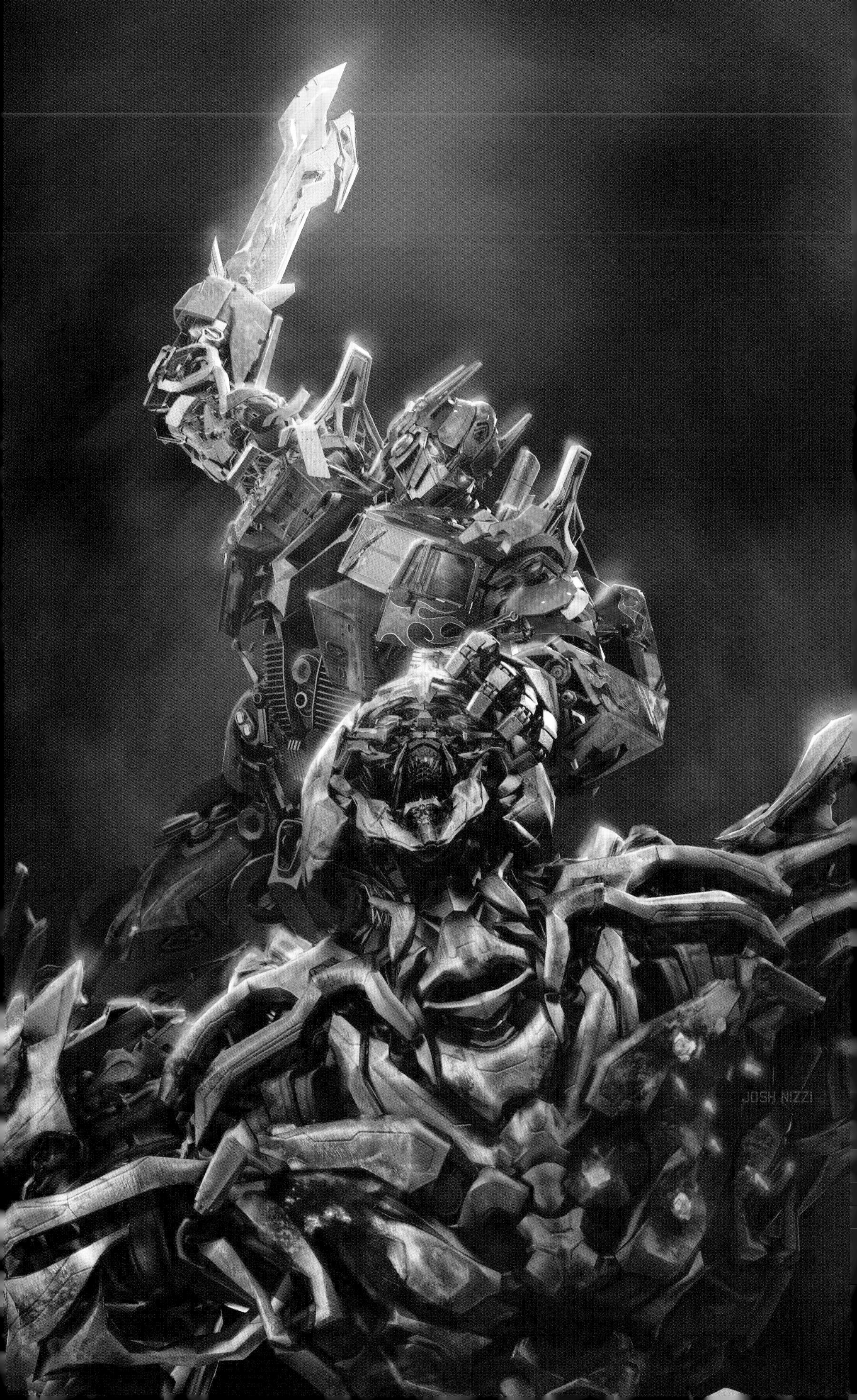
JOSH NIZZI

EXCLUSIVE MATERIAL

From concept to cover: A glimpse into Issue One's cover from Alex Milne.

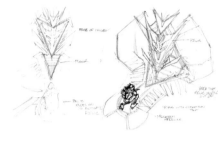

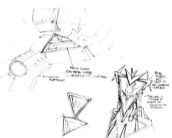

Various designs and layouts were used to show Megatron bowing before the mysterious relic discovered on Cybertron.

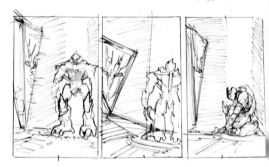

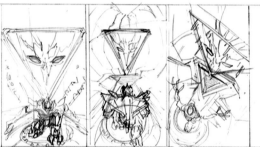

Inks for Alex Milne's incentive cover for Issue One.

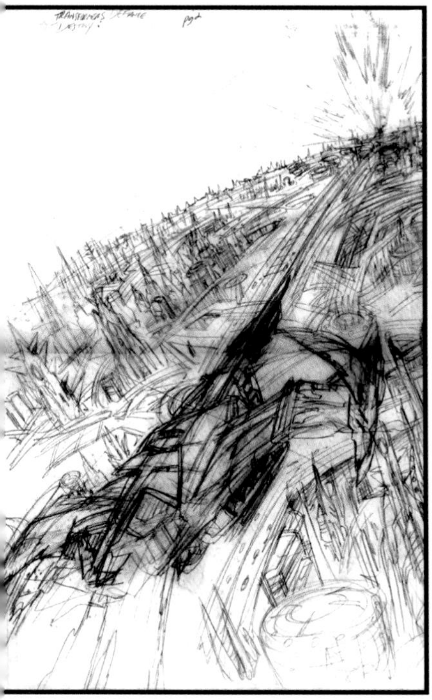

Issue One, page 2 rough sketch by Dan Khanna.

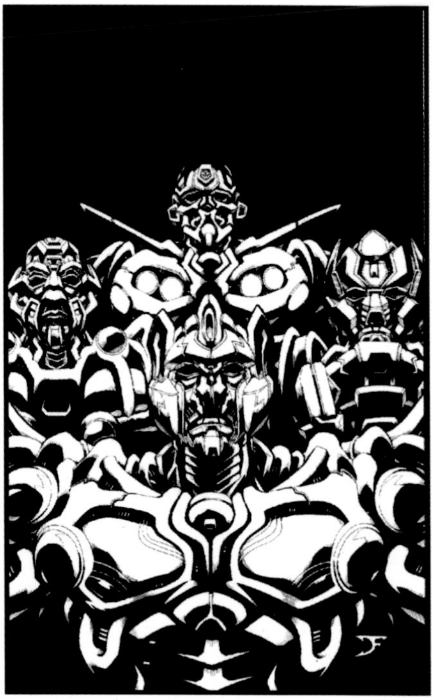

Inks for Issue Three's cover by Don Figueroa.
The cover is an homage to the band Queen.

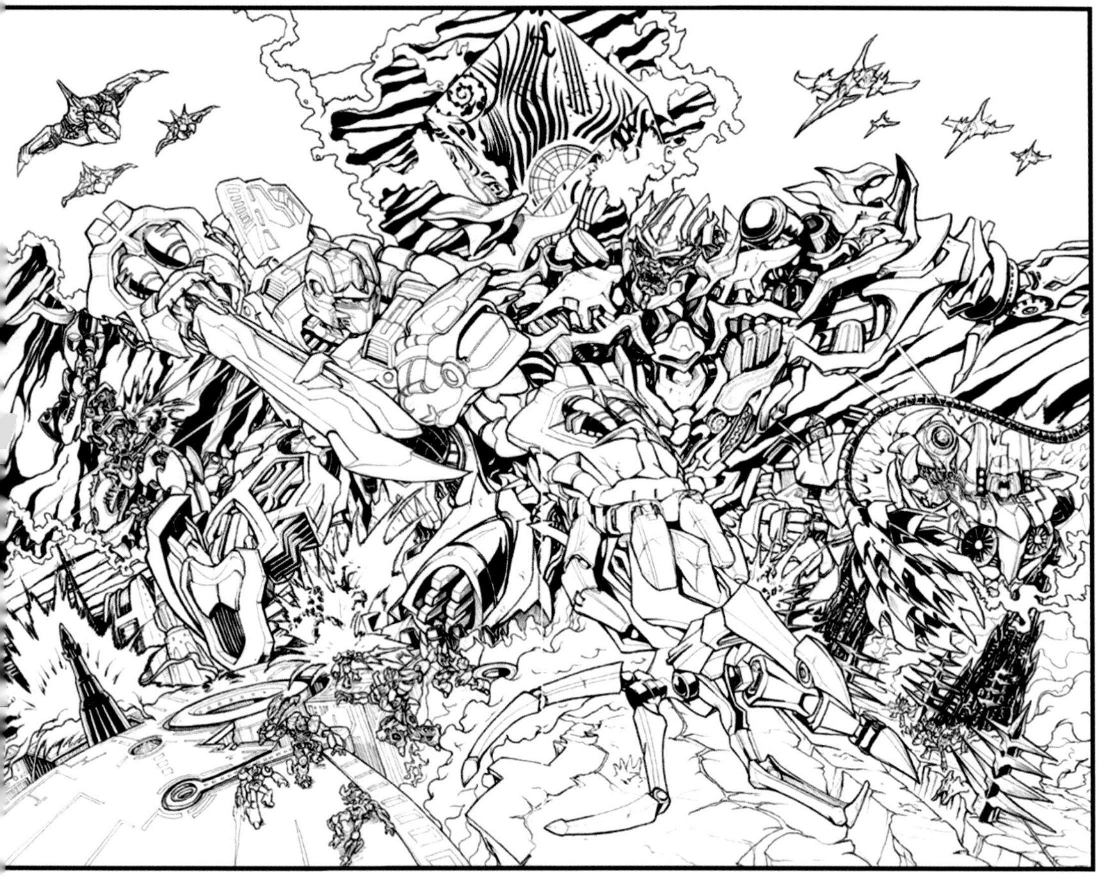

Original inks for Issue Four, pages 16–17 by Andrew Griffith.
These pages were altered to remove Megatron's mace weapon, as it appeared in the first film on his right arm.

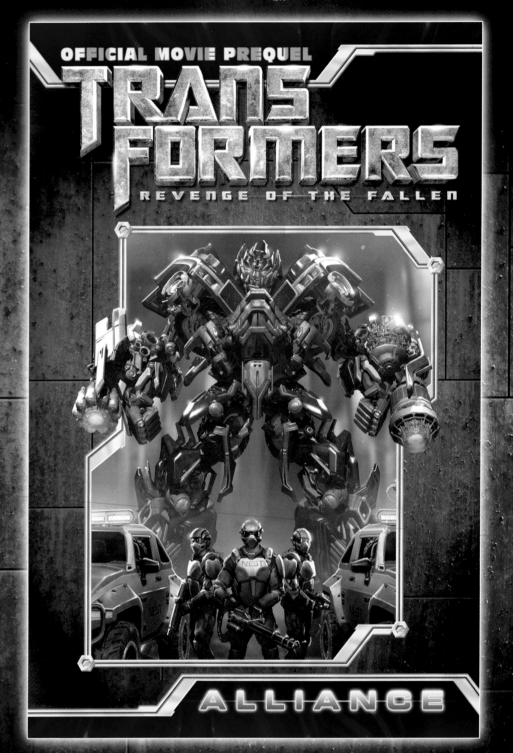